PALM READING SECRETS

A BEGINNER'S GUIDE TO PALMISTRY

Discover the secrets revealed by Roz Locke, Ph.D., in her exploration of Celebrity Palmist Nellie Simmons Meier's work.

ROZ LOCKE, PH.D.
& CYDNEY O'SULLIVAN

Palm Reading Secrets
A Beginners Guide to Palmistry
© 2023 Roz Locke Ph.D. & Cydney O'Sullivan All rights reserved.

No part of this publication may be reproduced or transmitted in any form or by any means, mechanical or electronic, including photocopying and recording, or by any information storage and retrieval system, without permission in writing from author or publisher (except by a reviewer, who may quote brief passages and/or show brief video clips in a review).

Limit of Liability/Disclaimer of Warranty: Whilst the publisher and author have used their best efforts in preparing this book, they make no representations or warranties with respect to the accuracy or completeness of the contents of this book and specifically disclaim any implied warranties of merchantability or fitness for a particular purpose. No warranty may be created or extended by sales representatives or written sales material. The advice and strategies contained herein is intended for a general audience and does not purport to be, nor should it be construed as, specific advice tailored to any individual and may not be suitable for your situation. You should consult with a professional adviser where appropriate.

There is no guarantee, express or implied, that you will earn any money using the techniques and ideas in this book. Examples in these materials are not to be interpreted as a promise or guarantee of earnings. Earning potential is entirely dependent on the efforts and skills of the person applying all or part of the concepts, ideas and strategies contained herein.

Neither the publisher nor the author shall be liable for any loss of profit or any other commercial damages, including but not limited to special, incidental, consequential, or other damages.

Palm Prints Courtesy of The Library of Congress

Published by Celebrity Publishers
www.CelebrityPublishers.com
USA +1 702 997 2229
Australia +61 2 8005 4878

PALM READING SECRETS
A BEGINNER'S GUIDE
TO PALMISTRY

Ever Dreamed of Unlocking the Mysteries in Your Palms – or Turning That Skill into Profit?

"Palm Reading Secrets: A Beginner's Guide to Palmistry" by Roz Locke, Ph.D., is not just a book; it's your first step into the fascinating world of palmistry, enriched by the wisdom of the legendary palmist Nellie Simmons Meier. This guide is more than a personal journey; it's a potential path to a lucrative career in palm reading.

Discover the Hidden Language of Your Life – For You and Others

Your palms are a unique narrative of your life, personality, and future. Roz Locke, a seasoned expert in palmistry, reveals these secrets in an engaging and accessible manner. This book isn't just about understanding your own palms; it's about acquiring a skill that could open doors to a new, profitable venture.

From Curiosity to Mastery to Earning!

Whether you're a beginner or someone with a budding interest in palmistry, this guide is your comprehensive mentor. It takes you from the basics of understanding palm reading lines to mastering the art of interpretation. Imagine the possibility of turning this newfound skill into a thriving business, offering insights and guidance to others.

Learn from the Best, Earn Like the Rest.

Roz Locke brings the teachings of celebrity palmist Nellie Simmons Meier right to your fingertips, blending ancient wisdom with practical business insights. This book is your bridge to not only learning an age-old art but also understanding how to monetize this skill in today's world.

A Journey of Personal and Professional Discovery

Palm reading is more than a hobby; it's a tool for self-discovery and a potential business opportunity. Picture yourself gaining deep personal insights and using this knowledge to carve out a unique, profitable niche in the market.

Why Wait? Start Your Palmistry Business Journey Today

Your palms hold stories waiting to be told, and "Palm Reading Secrets: A Beginner's Guide to Palmistry" is the key to unlocking these tales. This book is more than an investment; it's your gateway to a journey of self-discovery, knowledge, and potential financial success.

EXCLUSIVE BONUS OFFER FOR READERS

Unlock the Mysteries of Palmistry with Our Special Offer!

Dear Reader of Palm Reading Secrets,

You've embarked on an exciting journey into the world of palmistry with our book. Are you ready to dive even deeper? We have an exclusive invitation just for you!

Introducing the "Palm Reading Secrets Course" – Your Gateway to Mastering Palmistry

Experience Palmistry Like Never Before

Join our comprehensive online course designed to take your palm reading skills to the next level. Whether you're a curious beginner or an aspiring palmist, this course is the perfect next step in your journey.

Why Join the Palm Reading Secrets Course?

1. **In-Depth Training**: Delve into advanced techniques and interpretations that go beyond the book. Learn to read palms with greater accuracy and insight.

2. **Expert Guidance:** Be guided by seasoned palmists. Our instructors bring years of experience and will share their secret tips and tricks with you.

3. **More Insights from Celebrity Palm Reader Nellie Simmons Meier:** Access hundreds of palm reading sessions meticulously detailed by Mrs Meier to practice and perfect your skills.

4. **Exclusive Community Access:** Connect with fellow palmistry enthusiasts. Share readings, gain feedback, and grow together in a supportive environment.

Special Bonus Offer – Free Trial Access!

As a valued reader of "Palm Reading Secrets," we're thrilled to offer you a FREE trial to access the **Palm Reading Secrets** Course.

Your Free Trial Includes:

- Full access to the first module of the course.
- Early bird discounts on the full course upon completion of your trial.

Embrace Your Palmistry Passion

This is your chance to enhance your understanding and skills in palmistry. With our course, you'll gain the confidence to read palms like a pro and uncover the secrets hidden in the lines of the hand.

Don't Miss This Opportunity!

Claim your free trial now and continue your journey into the fascinating world of palmistry.

Your path to palmistry mastery awaits. Join the **Palm Reading Secrets Course** today and unlock the full potential of your palm reading abilities!

From Curiosity to Mastery to Earning!

Whether you're a beginner or someone with a budding interest in palmistry, this course is your comprehensive mentoring program. It takes you from the basics of understanding palm reading lines to mastering the art of interpretation. Imagine the possibility of turning this newfound skill into a thriving business, offering insights and guidance to others.

LEARN PALM READING SECRETS
A Beginner's Guide to Palmistry
ROZ LOCKE, Ph.D.

BONUS FREE TRIAL MEMBERSHIP

Discover the Secrets Revealed by Roz Locke, Ph.D., in her Exploration of Celebrity Palmist Nellie Simmons Meier's Work.

Here's how to get access:
https://PalmReadingSecrets.com/ReaderBonuses

DEDICATION

I Dedicate this book to my Sons, Jeffrey Alan and Edward (Eki) Locke, who make me proud every day and have given me a trunk full of love, support, humor, kindness, gratitude and fantastic memories, to borrow when needed, for a lifetime.

And to the fascinating Nellie Simmons Meier for sharing her knowledge and expertise so generously with the world, inspiring me to do the same.

ACKNOWLEDGEMENTS

I'd like to thank the dedicated collectors of the archives of Nellie Simmons Meier who helped provide invaluable insights during my extensive research of her life.

I'd also like to extend my gratitude to my publishing team Celebrity Publishers for helping me turn all this knowledge into a book and courses.

ABOUT THE AUTHORS

Roz Locke, Ph.D., embodies a life rich in diversity and achievement, making her journey through life nothing short of extraordinary. Her unique blend of insatiable curiosity, keen intelligence, and a relentlessly positive outlook has led her to explore a vast array of experiences.

Her proudest achievement lies in raising two sons who have grown into confident, compassionate, and thoughtful individuals.

Her academic journey began remarkably early, entering college at just 16 and swiftly earning her bachelor's degree. This early success fueled her passion for exploring unconventional knowledge, leading her to delve into the fascinating world of Palmistry. Driven by questions about its history, the potential to decipher life stories from palm lines, and the deeper meanings behind these ancient practices, she embarked on a journey of discovery.

Her quest for knowledge didn't stop there. Dr. Locke expanded her expertise by earning an MBA, a Doctorate in Holistic Health, and certifications in herbalism, Zone therapy from the Qi Gong Institute of China, and as a Reiki master teacher. She also made her mark as the first Reiki practitioner at Queens Medical Center in Honolulu, Hawaii. Her entrepreneurial spirit shone through as a pastry chef, delighting the Hamptons, NY, with her exquisite desserts.

Her commitment to service is as profound as her academic pursuits. From her teenage years volunteering at a veterans hospital to her involvement in Dr. Martin Luther King's Poor People's Campaign, her dedication to making a difference is unwavering. She has spent over two decades securing medical supplies for Sierra Leone, West Africa, and serving on the board of the Guinea Development Foundation, significantly impacting women and children's lives in Guinea Conakry.

Her journey led her to the remarkable Nellie Simmons Meier, a renowned palmist to the stars and influential figures of her time, including President Franklin Delano Roosevelt. Dr. Locke's exhaustive research into Meier's life and work, including a visit to Meier's perfectly preserved home, forms the foundation of her book, "Palm Reading Secrets."

Cydney O'Sullivan, an accomplished professional writer and 18-time best-selling author, was thrilled to have the pleasure of collaborating with Roz Locke on a book project that delves into the fascinating world of palmistry. As the founder of Celebrity Publishers, Cydney is renowned for her passion for bringing compelling stories to life, and this collaboration was no exception. Her enthusiasm for storytelling shines through in her work, especially in projects that explore intriguing subjects like the life and legacy of the remarkable Nellie Simmons Meier.

Nellie Simmons Meier's work in the field of palmistry is not just a topic of interest but a profound legacy that Cydney was eager to explore and share with a broader audience. Her expertise in authorship and publishing played a pivotal role in effectively organizing and presenting the essence of Meier's groundbreaking work in palmistry. Through this collaboration, Cydney aimed to shed light on the scientific aspects and the rich experiences that defined Meier's career, making it accessible and engaging for readers worldwide.

This collaboration is more than just a literary endeavor for Cydney; it's an opportunity to bring to light the intricate blend of science and experience that palmistry embodies, as seen through the life and work of Nellie Simmons Meier.

Palm Reading Secrets is not just a book; it's a culmination of scholarly research and practical wisdom from one of America's leading Palmistry experts. It draws extensively from the detailed archives of Nellie Simmons Meier, a celebrity palm reader whose scientific approach to palmistry was enhanced by her psychic intuition. This book is a treasure trove of knowledge, offering insights into the lives of many of the famous clients Meier served while standing as a cornerstone guide in the art of Palmistry.

TABLE OF CONTENTS

Foreword xvii

Prologue xix

    Case Study: Eleanor Roosevelt xxix

Introduction 1

    Case Study: Walt Disney 7

The Basics of Palmistry 11

    Case Study: Lowell Thomas 19

The Power of Palm Reading 31

The Four Hand Types 57

    Case Study: George Gershwin 73

The Major Lines 77

    Case Study: Margaret Sanger 81

The Minor Lines 85

    Case Study: Amelia Earhart 89

The Mounts 93

    Case Study: Alexander, Grand Duke of Russia 103

Finger Analysis 107

    Case Study: Marie, Grand Duchess of Russia 114

Special Markings and Symbols 119

    Case Study: Booker T. Washington 123

Putting It All Together 125

    Case Study: Susan B. Anthony 137

Ethical Considerations in Palmistry 141
    Case Study: Leslie Howard 146
Advanced Techniques and Further Study 149
    Case Study: Mary Pickford 162
Beyond Palm Reading: Integrating Numerology
and Astrology 167
    Case Study: Walter Huston 175
Preserving the Art of Palmistry. 177
    Case Study:
    Pu Lun Prince of China 180
Acknowledging the Legacy of Nellie Simmons Meier 183

FOREWORD

Have you ever wondered why you are the way you are, or what your future holds?

In the enchanting realm of palmistry, where the lines on one's hand whisper secrets of the past, present, and future, "Palm Reading Secrets: A Beginner's Guide to Palmistry" emerges as a beacon of knowledge and insight. Authored by the distinguished Roz Locke, PhD, this book is a tribute to the timeless wisdom of celebrity palmist Nellie Simmons Meier, whose work has fascinated and inspired countless and many celebrity individuals across the globe for almost a century.

As you turn the pages of this comprehensive guide, you embark on a journey that transcends mere curiosity. This book is a vessel carrying the rich legacy of Nellie Simmons Meier, whose profound understanding of palmistry has illuminated the paths of many seeking clarity and direction. Roz Locke, with her eloquent writing and deep knowledge, serves as the perfect guide to lead you through the intricate and mesmerizing world of palm reading.

Palmistry is an art form that dates back thousands of years, a practice steeped in mystery and allure. It is a language spoken by the hands, where every line, curve, and mark holds the potential to reveal the chapters of one's life story. "Palm Reading Secrets" is meticulously crafted to demystify this language, offering a clear and engaging approach to understanding the nuances of palm reading lines. Whether it's the heart line speaking of love and relationships or the life line narrating personal vitality and life changes, this book ensures you grasp the essence of each.

What sets this guide apart is its harmonious blend of theoretical knowledge and practical application. It is richly adorned with illustrations and step-by-step instructions, making the ancient practice of palm reading accessible and enjoyable for everyone. From the curious beginner to the enthusiastic learner, this book caters to all, ensuring that the art of palm reading is not just learned but experienced.

Roz Locke's work is a tribute to the legacy of Nellie Simmons Meier, ensuring that her insights and expertise continue to enlighten the minds of those drawn to the world of palmistry. As you delve into this book, you are not just learning to read palms; you are stepping into a journey of self-discovery and understanding, a journey that promises to reveal the secrets hidden in the palm of your hand.

"Palm Reading Secrets: A Beginner's Guide to Palmistry" is more than a book; it is a gateway to a new perspective, a tool for introspection, and a means to connect with others on a deeper level. Embrace this journey with an open mind and heart, and let the ancient wisdom of palmistry guide you towards a greater understanding of yourself and the world around you.

Sylvie Taylor Young Ph.D.
Clinical Psychologist

PROLOGUE

"Very well, you Doubting Thomas, let us journey back into Time, a long way back, and visit no less a personage than Aristotle. In the year 350 B.C. we find that great philosopher engaged in writing a work to be known to posterity, even to this day, as "Aristotle's Masterpiece." And in this Masterpiece there is one complete chapter -

"Of Palmistry, showing the various
Judgements drawn from the hand."

At the conclusion of the chapter appears this verse:

"Thus he that Nature rightly understands,
May from each Line imprinted in his Hands,
His future Fate and Fortune come to know,
And what Path it is his Feet shall go.
His Secret Inclinations he may see,
And to what Vice he shall addicted be
To th' End that when he looks into his Hand,
He may upon his Guard the better stand;
And turn his wandering Steps another way:
When e'er he finds he does from Virtue stray."

– **Nellie Simmons Meier
Excerpt From Lions' Paws, The Story of Famous Hands**

Celebrating a Trailblazer: Nellie Simmons Meier

Shortly after moving to Indianapolis, I met an artist who told me about a woman from the area who read palms for famous people many years ago. He also told me that her house had been bought by a man named Kenneth Keene, and that he had kept the house pretty much the way it was, and that it was a very interesting place. The artist had been to the house to attend a party.

The palm reader's name was Nellie Simmons Meier (NSM) and that was the beginning of my quest to find out more about who this fascinating person was. I visited Kenneth Keene at his home and found him to be a delightful and interesting storyteller. There were several palm prints of famous people on the walls, and Mr. Keene said he had tried to keep the house in the same era as when Nellie Simmons Meier lived there.

I began to spend several hours a day after my work, researching and finding out as much as possible about this interesting woman who lived in a midwest town during the early 1900's through the 1920', 1930's and up until her death in 1944. She certainly was not the typical woman of that time, many of whom married by the age of 20 years old, more probably in her teens, had children, stayed home and took care of her family.

Nellie Simmons Meier, born as Nellie Palmer Simmons on November 10, 1863, in Cohoes, New York, tied the knot with George Phillip Meier on February 14, 1899, in Indianapolis, Indiana. Both George and Nellie were close in age, with George being born on September 16, 1863, in Marshall, Michigan. At the time of their marriage, they were both 36 years old and did not have any children.

Interestingly, Nellie's parents, just like her and George, were the same age when they got married. Nellie's mother, Catherine Clinton Austin, was born on August 17, 1839, in Moreau, New York, and passed away in April 1897 in Indianapolis, Indiana, at the age of

58. Her father, Daniel Simmons, was born on February 8, 1839, in Trenton, New Jersey, and passed away on September 28, 1916, in Worcester, Massachusetts, at the age of 77. Catherine and Daniel had exchanged vows on June 21, 1859, in Moreau, New York, when they were both 20 years old.

Nellie and George Meier left a notable mark in history. George Philip Meier was a prominent designer of women's apparel during the early 20th century in the United States and abroad. He believed that clothing was not merely attire but an expression of the wearer's artistic sensibility.

Born to German immigrants in Marshall, Michigan, George moved to Indianapolis in 1898. There, he established a successful women's tailoring and dressmaking business in his home at 962 North Pennsylvania Street. He married Nellie Simmons, a palm reader, on Valentine's Day in 1899.

George Meier's exceptional tailoring skills and artistic design sensibilities propelled him to fame in Indianapolis. His reputation led him to become a designer for L. S. AYRES & COMPANY just three years after opening his shop. In 1905, with the opening of Ayres' new multistory building, George was given a significant portion of the store's custom dressmaking space for his own business. Eventually, he became the chief fashion designer and foreign buyer for the company.

George and Nellie also became prominent art patrons and social figures in Indianapolis, hosting gatherings that attracted famous writers, artists, actors, dancers, and musicians. Their lives were intertwined with the art and fashion world of their time, leaving an indelible legacy in the history of fashion and culture.

I tell you all of this because as we explore the realm of palmistry, in this book and companion training programs I wanted to share some of the tremendous contributions made by Nellie Simmons Meier, a remarkable figure who significantly enriched the field with her groundbreaking work.

Nellie was a renowned American palmist and astrologer, known for her contributions to the field of palmistry and her work in spreading its popularity during the late 19th and early 20th centuries.

While she gained popularity and had a successful career as a palmist, historical records and sources from that time are not detailed enough to provide a comprehensive list of famous individuals who sought her services. Additionally, privacy concerns and the nature of palmistry consultations make it challenging to ascertain the exact identities of her clients.

For example, we know from archives that Nellie Simmons Meier was engaged by Eleanor Roosevelt to read the palms of herself and her husband, beloved 32nd President of the United States, Franklin Delanor Roosevelt, along with several other important people at the White House at that time. However, by their request she agreed to never share the FDR readings publicly .

Through my research, and thanks to Joseph J. Plaud, who founded the Franklin Delanor Roosevelt Heritage Center, Inc., I discovered many insights into the Roosevelt readings.

From the depths of the archives came a treasure trove of history – the FDR collection, featuring the original, signed handprints of Franklin and Eleanor Roosevelt, complete with detailed palmistry readings. This remarkable collection, sold by auction some years ago, was a true gem of intimacy and historical significance. It included the original Roosevelt handprints, each accompanied by full character sketches based on the autographed impressions analyzed by Nellie Simmons Meier.

This extraordinary collection also housed the original, autographed handprints of various Roosevelt family members, two vice presidents, and other key figures from the Roosevelt administration. The collection was further enriched by four original letters penned by Eleanor Roosevelt and one by Stephen T. Early, the Secretary to the President, all dating back to the fall of 1937. These letters, referencing Mrs. Meier's visit to the White House, offer a glimpse into the historical context of these readings, along with copies of Mrs. Meier's responses.

Included in this collection is Mrs. Meier's unpublished study on the Roosevelts, the first page of which is a testament to the unique characteristics she observed in the family's handprints. She noted, "Rarely have I looked in the hands of a family where outstanding characteristics seem to have been handed down, literally, from father, mother to children."

The story of how these handprints came to be is as fascinating as the prints themselves. Initially, it was Eleanor Roosevelt who arranged a meeting with Mrs. Meier. However, after her session, the intrigue spread rapidly through the White House. On February 26, 1937, Mrs. Meier visited the White House for a private session with Eleanor, and before she left, she had also read the palms of several other family members and close associates. This event led to a scheduled return on March 1st, 1937, for a session with FDR and his political confidants.

In total, Mrs. Meier took 24 original handprints, both right and left hands, of 12 individuals within the White House. These handprints formed the core of this incredible collection, offering a unique insight into the first family and their close associates.

The interpretations of these handprints are profound. Mrs. Meier's 13-page analysis of FDR's palms speaks volumes of his character, noting his wide range of ideas, great vitality, and ease of accomplishment. Eleanor Roosevelt's 11-page interpretation highlighted her civic duty, altruism, and appreciation for the arts. Accompanying these analyses are five typed letters, three on official White House stationery, discussing the use of Mrs. Meier's readings in her future publications.

The correspondence between Mrs. Meier and the White House is particularly telling. In a letter dated October 7th, 1937, Eleanor Roosevelt expressed concern over the release of the President's handprints and character analysis during his tenure in the White

House. Stephen T. Early's letter, dated October 11th, 1937, reiterated this stance, outlining the conditions under which the material could be released.

Mrs. Meier's respectful responses to both letters assured that she would not publish any material without the President's approval and consent. These exchanges underscore the sensitivity and significance of the handprints and character sketches within the context of FDR's presidency.

The handprints and accompanying documents in this collection are not just historical artifacts; they represent a unique intersection of personal, political, and mystical worlds. Nellie Simmons Meier's interest in the hands of famous individuals, as showcased in her 1937 bestseller "Lions' Paws," is a testament to her belief in palmistry as a window into human character and destiny.

The papers of Nellie Simmons Meier, donated to the Library of Congress in 1938, add another layer of historical value to this collection. The significance of these items historically for the broader public, is immeasurable. They offer a rare and intimate glimpse into the lives of many of the world's most influential people and the unique perspective of a renowned palmist of the era.

Franklin Delanor Roosevelt aside, I was able to obtain over 2000 palm prints that Nellie Simmons Meier recorded during her career and have included insights in this book from the readings of some of the most influential people of the era.

Another fascinating story I came upon in my research was about the renowned actress Carole Lombard. It has been said that she sought the guidance of Nellie Simmons Meier, concerned about her marriage to the iconic actor Clark Gable. According to the legend, Nellie reassured Lombard that her marriage was stable, but advised her not to hurry back.

Tragically, Lombard, insistent on traveling, boarded a TWA DC-3 in Las Vegas along with her mother, Elizabeth Peters, MGM publicity agent Otto Winkler, and 15 young Army pilots. Shortly after takeoff, the aircraft tragically deviated from its course. Due to wartime blackout precautions against potential Japanese air attacks, navigational beacons were turned off, leading the plane to crash into a cliff near Potosi Mountain's summit.

Carole Lombard, only 33 years old at the time of the accident, was laid to rest beside her mother. Her grave is marked with an epitaph that reads "Carole Lombard Gable." It's been said by many who knew him that Clark Gable never got over losing her and when he died in 1960 he was laid to rest beside her.

It is important to note that celebrities and notable figures often seek the guidance of various practitioners, including palmists, astrologers, and psychics, both past and present. While her work was influential and widely respected, her specific interactions with celebrities might not be as well-documented as her overall contributions to the field of palmistry.

In this section, we pay homage to the life and legacy of Nellie Simmons Meier, an influential palmist of her time, whose dedication and expertise continue to inspire generations of practitioners. We unravel the key concepts and techniques she introduced, which have become indispensable in modern palmistry.

Nellie's Early Life and Passion for Palmistry

Nellie Simmons Meier, born in the late 19th century, was destined to leave an indelible mark on the world of palmistry. Raised in a family that valued spirituality and metaphysical pursuits, she developed a fascination with the mysteries of life from a young age. Her early exposure to astrology, numerology, and palmistry kindled a deep passion for the occult sciences, particularly palm reading.

Her interest in palmistry intensified as she grew older, and she began studying and practicing the art with unyielding enthusiasm. She dedicated countless hours to honing her skills, poring over ancient texts, and conducting extensive research to expand her knowledge.

The Influence of Cheiro and Other Masters

Among Nellie Simmons Meier's influential sources of inspiration was the renowned palmist and astrologer, William John Warner, popularly known as Cheiro. Cheiro's works, including "Cheiro's Language of the Hand" and "You and Your Hand," deeply influenced her understanding of palmistry. His system of palm reading, coupled with her personal insights and experiences, paved the way for her to develop her unique approach to hand analysis.

In addition to Cheiro, she drew wisdom from other esteemed palmistry practitioners and metaphysical pioneers of her time. It is said she delved into the writings of Richard Saunders, Dr Charlotte Wolff, and Captain Casimir Stanislas D'Arpentigny, among others, absorbing diverse perspectives to enrich her palmistry practice.

Contributions to the Field of Palmistry

Nellie Simmons Meier's passion and dedication to palmistry led her to become one of the most respected and accomplished palmists of her era. Her innate ability to read hands, coupled with her keen intuition and profound insights, enabled her to offer accurate and enlightening readings to her clients.

In addition to her successful palmistry practice, she was an avid writer and educator.

Pioneering Systematic Hand Analysis

One of Nellie Simmons Meier's most significant contributions to the field of palmistry was her development of a structured and systematic approach to hand analysis. Drawing from her extensive research and personal insights, she devised a comprehensive method that allowed for a detailed examination of the hand's lines, mounts, and features.

Her systematic approach emphasized the interconnectedness of the various elements in hand analysis. She understood that each line and mark on the hand held a unique story, and it was the integration of these individual stories that offered a complete understanding of the individual's personality, potential, and life journey.

Ethical Practice and Empowerment

Beyond her technical expertise, Nellie Simmons Meier was deeply committed to ethical palmistry practice. She believed that palmistry should be used responsibly, with a focus on empowering individuals rather than promoting fear or dependency. Her readings were characterized by compassion, understanding, and a sincere desire to help her clients gain insights into their lives and make informed decisions.

Throughout her career, she emphasized the importance of free will and personal responsibility. She encouraged her clients to use the knowledge gained from palmistry as a tool for self-awareness and growth, rather than a fixed prophecy of their destinies.

Her Legacy and Influence on Modern Palmistry

Nellie Simmons Meier's contributions to the field of palmistry continue to resonate with contemporary practitioners and enthusiasts alike. Her legacy lives on through the countless palmists she inspired and mentored, each carrying forward her dedication to the art and her commitment to ethical practice.

Her systematic approach to hand analysis remains a cornerstone of modern palmistry, and her book continues to serve as a valuable resource for aspiring palmists seeking to deepen their understanding of this ancient art.

As we celebrate her pioneering spirit and unwavering passion for palmistry, we honor her as a trailblazer whose work continues to enlighten and empower seekers of wisdom from the lines of the hand. The journey she embarked upon in unraveling the secrets held within the human palm serves as an enduring inspiration for all those who seek to unlock the profound mysteries of life through the art of palmistry.

Throughout this book we have included several enlightening celebrity palm readings shared in her notes and best selling book **Lions' Paws**, published in 1937.

CASE STUDY: ELEANOR ROOSEVELT

"The First Lady"

Eleanor Roosevelt, upon entering the White House in 1933, modestly described herself as "plain, ordinary Mrs. Roosevelt," yet proved to be an exceptional First Lady. She broke new ground by hosting the first-ever press conference for female reporters in 1933, and in 1939, famously resigned from the Daughters of the American Revolution to protest racial discrimination.

Throughout her husband's presidency, Eleanor was a vital link, extensively touring the nation, inspecting living and working conditions, and relaying her findings to President Roosevelt. Known as his "eyes, ears, and legs," she played a crucial role in ensuring the continuation of New Deal principles during WWII. A champion for the underprivileged, minorities, and the disadvantaged, Eleanor captivated the public with her daily column, "My Day," from 1935 until her death in 1962. During WWII, she also contributed as Assistant Director of Civilian Defense and uplifted Allied spirits through visits to England and the South Pacific.

Adapted from The Character Sketch From Hand Impressions of Mrs. Franklin Delanor Roosevelt (Eleanor Roosevelt) by Nellie Simmons Meier

People arrived skeptical but left as believers...

Nellie Simmons Meier had long been eager to capture the hand impressions of Eleanor Roosevelt. Finally, through the assistance of a mutual acquaintance, the opportunity presented itself.

Mrs. Roosevelt greeted her warmly, extending her hand in a friendly manner. Her hands, broad at the base of the fingers and tapering towards the wrist, revealed not just a remarkable adaptability in thought and action, but also an affinity for the arts and an appreciation for beauty in nature and her environment. This hand type suggests a restlessness, both mentally and physically, often moving from one activity to another with equal enthusiasm and interest. Her palm indicated a blend of traits, with altruism being the predominant one. Her physical vigor matched the pace of her extraordinary intellectual pursuits.

Her thought process did not reflect that of a contemplative philosopher. In her haste to see outcomes, she almost outpaced her own progress, allowing little time to achieve the objectives she envisioned. The adage "you can lead a horse to water, but you can't make it drink" seemed irrelevant to her. Driven by a sincere wish to better the conditions of those she cared about, she assumed they shared her eagerness to embrace the improvements she believed would benefit them. Mrs. Roosevelt's public life was more widely recognized than it was comprehended or sometimes valued.

The length of her fingers' phalanges generally indicated a dedicated commitment to her duties as she perceived them. She adhered strictly to her principles, "letting the chips fall where they may," unconcerned about personal repercussions if she believed her actions were justified. Her palm was soft yet firm, suggesting she was receptive to new ideas and impressions, even through a simple handshake. She was quick to discern the underlying intentions of a handshake, yet it never deterred her from her resolute goals.

Her fingers spread out like a starfish. The broad spread of her thumb denoted an abundance of both mental and physical activity, and an extraordinary level of nervous energy. She appeared to place no limits on her physical endurance or the time she devoted to others. Her spontaneous generosity was remarkable. The wide gap between her first and second fingers highlighted her independent nature, making her a rule unto herself. She brushed aside traditional norms, current societal constraints, and potential future complexities. The significant gap between her second and third fingers illustrated her complete disregard for the proverbial "rainy day."

For her, the immediate need was paramount. This distinctiveness also revealed her originality, which was evident in everything she said and did. The separation of her little finger from the hand indicated her strong independence in action, her quick-wittedness, and depth of thought, leading me to describe her as an intelligent, intellectual acrobat. She was forthright in her expression, both verbally and in writing, often speaking without hesitation. To her, situations were clear-cut, prompting immediate responses, yet she sometimes overlooked the essential fact that minds need to be ready to accept new ideas for them to truly take root. Her long fingers were indicative of her attention to detail, not so much in personal comfort or attire, but driven by a strong sense of duty, which prioritized the needs of others over her own. Her selflessness often made others seem selfish in comparison, due to her relentless efforts to enhance their lives.

Her elongated first finger demonstrated remarkable executive skills, allowing her to meticulously plan her days and nights. Even in social settings, seemingly for her enjoyment, her primary concern was the happiness she could bring to others. The pointed tip of her first finger, with its rapid perception, was like a cutting torch, swiftly clearing obstacles and grasping the essence of issues. However, her quick judgments were often colored by her sympathies and interests, leading her to conclusions based more on personal perspectives than on neutral, unbiased reasoning. The first segment of this finger, representing compassion, was significantly longer than the second, symbolizing justice. This meant she leaned towards mercy, sometimes at the expense of the necessary justice that reinforces the value of mercy. Excessive leniency can be more detrimental than strict justice, as the latter teaches the hard lessons of transgression, while the former might imply a lack of consequences.

For her, discipline was more a theoretical concept and a matter of suggestion than of personal enforcement. The rounded tip of her second finger reflected her physical, mental, and spiritual resilience. In her dynamic lexicon, retreat was not an option. The length of the nail phalange suggested her motives and goals were altruistic. While the Salvation Army's motto is, "man may be down, but he is never out," hers seemed to be, "man is never down, only in need of guidance."

The extended second phalange indicated a wisdom necessary to temper her diverse activities, though this often came as an afterthought. The long third phalange represented her "love of the land," her affection for home and its surroundings, and her capability to manage domestic affairs. The extended nail phalange of the third finger showed her preference for lines, form, and structure over color in her appreciation of creative arts. The pointed tip revealed her love for idealism, and with her broad sense of charity, she evaluated others' creative, professional, or commercial efforts more by their intentions than by their achievements.

The third phalange also highlighted her knack for assessing commercial value. Yet, her analytical approach was frequently overridden by her eagerness to support or inspire others.

The pronounced separation of the fourth finger, representing Mercury, from the hand was quite remarkable. The breadth of mental and physical activities she engaged in was so vast that restraint in speech or action was seldom seen, especially when her judgment was swayed by her deep sympathy and her intense desire to bring joy to others from her perspective. This inclination was further amplified by her vivid imagination, as indicated by the headline drooping towards the Mount of the Moon. The first segment of the fourth finger was notably dominant over the other two. Its length signified her strong communicative abilities, while its pointed tip revealed her tactfulness in handling various matters.

She was adept at multitasking, capable of dictating talks and speeches even amidst physical activities, though she heavily relied on her secretary for transcribing her speeches and public communications. Her fingers' flexibility mirrored her mental adaptability, evident in her interest in diverse activities and her empathetic understanding of others' opportunities and challenges. However, her optimistic nature, as suggested by the pointed tip of her second finger, and her eagerness to see others succeed often led her to underestimate their lack of readiness, which was crucial for their success.

Discussing her thumb, it's important to highlight its role as a cornerstone in character formation. The thumb revealed the potential for success through the application of willpower guided by logic, or the possibility of failure due to its absence. Mrs. Roosevelt's thumb was particularly intriguing, displaying traits that seemed contradictory. Generally, its length and position on the hand suggested a willpower applied intelligently, with an awareness of the consequences. Yet, it's pronounced flare from the hand, denoting a strong sense of independence, sometimes proved to be a hindrance.

Her thumb brought to Nellie's mind the adage, "one can go all wrong by trying too hard to go all right." The longer first phalange of the thumb, representing willpower, compared to the shorter second phalange, indicative of logic and reason, suggested a propensity to act impulsively and reflect later. The first phalange, akin to the head of a hammer, and the second, its handle, implied that the latter was not robust enough to guide the former effectively; her emotional drive to help others often clouded her judgment regarding cause and effect.

The flexibility of her thumb further highlighted her generous nature, manifesting in her liberal expenditure of time, energy, and finances, traits also suggested by the thumb's flare. The third phalange, commonly known as the Mount of Venus, reflected her inherent kindness and expansive benevolence. Her ability to connect with "all sorts and conditions of people," as implied by her flexible thumb, was somewhat tempered by her "mental world," symbolized by the middle phalanges of all her fingers. This balancing influence was also evident in the first half of the headline in her right hand, which was straight enough to provide guidance and direction to the imaginative slope in her left hand. This balance was crucial in her involvement and support for the underprivileged. She clearly understood the impracticality of immersing herself in groups or situations that contradicted her core principles and personal standards of right living. However, she did not impose her own conventional beliefs and limitations on others.

The prominence of the Mount of Jupiter suggested a fondness for power and recognition, yet these traits were secondary to the dominant first phalange of conscience. Beneath Jupiter in her right hand, a star indicated her connections with notable and distinguished individuals, which was to be expected. The headline in her left hand sloped significantly towards the Mount of the Moon, indicating judgment influenced by imagination, somewhat restrained by the less pronounced slope in her right hand. While she maintained tolerance for differing viewpoints and was open to ideas reflecting similar altruism, she had developed the capacity to realistically confront the realities that led to the failure of her valued projects.

The headline in her left hand displayed a significant break, signifying a mental shock related to emotional matters. The clearly defined square of preservation surrounding this break allowed her to continue her mental pursuits, as evidenced by the uninterrupted flow of thought in the headline of her right hand. Additionally, a trident formation was present under the third finger of her right hand, with its three lines converging in the center.

This indicated her advancement in three key areas: business, literature, and charity, all converging into a single path that culminated at the heartline. It was evident, both in her actions and as seen in the termination of the heartline at the fork of loyalty and idealism, that her heart governed her mind. A notable feature in her hands was the presence of the medical stigmata, a small cluster of vertical lines beneath the fourth finger on the left hand.

ER naturally possessed the qualities of a "born nurse," instinctively knowing how to act in a medical emergency and capable of providing first aid calmly. Nellie recalled a personal anecdote here: that when she mentioned this trait, Franklin Jr., who was attentively following her analysis, interjected with a strong affirmation, recalling how his mother's presence alone made him feel better when he was ill in Boston.

The mark resembling the tip of a finger, almost like a glowing light bulb between the second and third fingers, symbolized the uplifting spirit of Apollo, the finger of art. However, this was tempered and grounded by the influence of the mount and finger of Saturn, ensuring that her cheerfulness and optimism were not fleeting but deeply ingrained and genuine, enabling her to face life's challenges with resilience.

When her actions were aligned with her deep-seated convictions and genuine sincerity, the line crossing the lower part of the Mount of the Moon indicated a phase of mental distress and worry, linked to a loved one struggling with addiction, a painful yet transient ordeal. The myriad of fine lines criss-crossing her palm, particularly in the left or 'history' hand, were testament to the trials, anxieties, and stresses she endured with remarkable bravery and an unyielding spirit, akin to a thoroughbred relentlessly pursuing its goal. In summary, regardless of one's personal alignment with her diverse interests, it was undeniable that Mrs. Roosevelt's actions were driven by absolute sincerity and a firm belief in the righteousness and justice of the causes she championed.

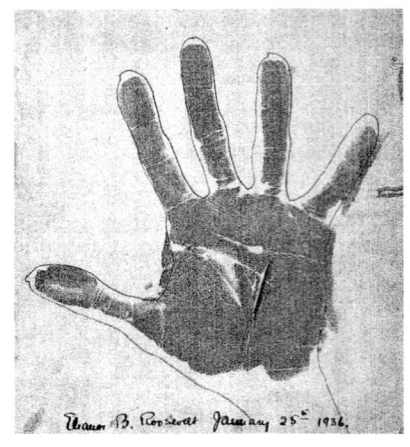

Left Hand Print 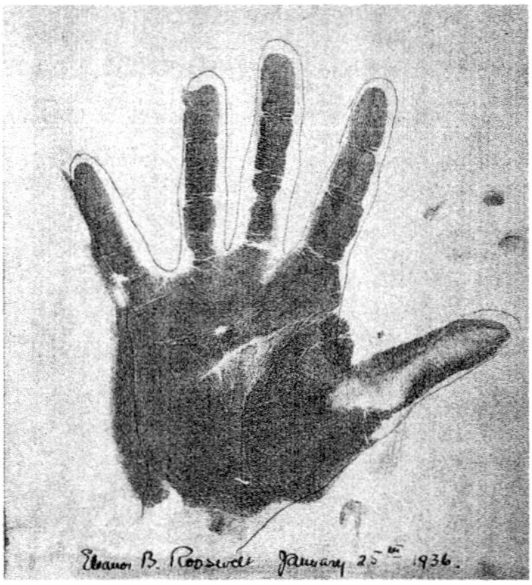   Right Hand Print

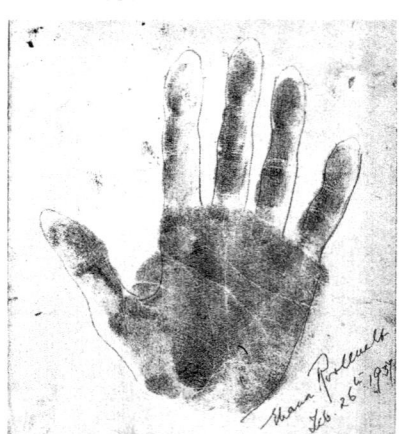

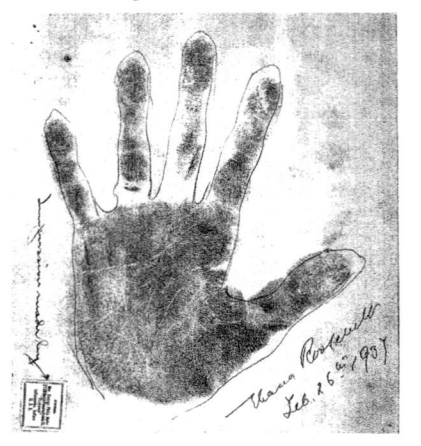

CHAPTER 1

Introduction

Welcome to the fascinating world of palmistry, where the lines etched upon the palms reveal profound insights into the human psyche and destiny. In this comprehensive guide we embark on a journey through the art and science of palm reading, exploring its rich history, timeless wisdom, and practical applications. Drawing inspiration from the pioneering work of Celebrity Palmist Nellie Simmons Meier, we delve deep into the intricacies of palmistry to equip you with the knowledge and skills needed to decipher the language of the hand.

In her book, Lions' Paws, Nellie Simmons Meier said for her it started with the handshake, this can give you your first insights into the very nature of a person. A firm, friendly grip will tell you on the simplest level they are open and fair, whereas, a fleeting touch of the fingertips extended in a perfunctory handshake says "you have definitely erected a wall between us, usually a wall of caste, which can be entered only through a door of equality, as you see equality."

The Ancient Art of Palmistry

Since time immemorial, human beings have sought to understand the mysteries of their existence and destiny. Palmistry, also known as chiromancy or palm reading, stands as one of the most ancient and revered forms of divination. Through the careful examination of the hand's lines, mounts, and features, palmistry offers a unique window into the individual's character, potential, and life path. We begin our journey by delving into the origins and evolution of palmistry, tracing its historical significance and cultural influences across different civilizations.

The Origins of Palmistry, Tracing The Ancient Roots

The art of palmistry, also known as chiromancy or cheiromancy, has a rich and complex history that spans multiple civilizations, each contributing its unique perspective and methodology to the practice. The universality of palmistry across different cultures and time periods suggests a deep-rooted fascination with the human hand as a key to understanding the self and the universe.

India: The Cradle of Palmistry

In India, palmistry is more than just a form of divination; it's a spiritual practice deeply embedded in the culture. Known as "hast samudrik shastra" or "palm samudrik," it is believed to have originated from the Vedic scriptures, which are among the oldest sacred texts in the world. The practice was considered so important that it was taught alongside other Vedic sciences like astrology and Ayurveda. The lines on the palm were not just seen as predictors of future events, but also as indicators of an individual's dharma (life purpose) and karma (actions and their consequences). The three major lines—life, heart, and head—were thought to offer insights into one's longevity, emotional disposition, and intellectual capabilities, respectively.

China: A Holistic Approach

In China, the practice of palmistry was closely linked with traditional Chinese medicine and the Taoist philosophy of balance and harmony. The Chinese approach to palmistry often involved a holistic reading that took into account not just the lines, but also the shapes, mounts, and even the color of the hand. This was believed to provide a more comprehensive understanding of an individual's health, character, and fate. The practice was often used in conjunction with other forms of Chinese divination like the I Ching, and it was not uncommon for Chinese physicians to use palmistry as a diagnostic tool.

Egypt: The Wisdom of the Nile

The ancient Egyptians were among the earliest practitioners of palmistry. Their interest in the human hand extended beyond mere fortune-telling; it was a form of wisdom and knowledge. The term "cheirognomy" comes from the Greek words "cheir" (hand) and "gnomon" (to know), and it was a practice that the Egyptians took very seriously. Hieroglyphics and artifacts suggest that palmistry was used for various purposes, including selecting priests, diagnosing diseases, and even in matters of statecraft. The practice was so revered that it was often depicted in art and literature, cementing its importance in ancient Egyptian culture.

Greece: Philosophical Underpinnings

In ancient Greece, palmistry was not just a mystical practice but was also studied and discussed by philosophers. Anaxagoras, a pre-Socratic philosopher, is said to have used palmistry to predict the rise of Cyrus the Great. The Greeks were particularly interested in the ethical and philosophical implications of palmistry. They believed that the hand, as an instrument of action, was a reflection of the individual's moral and intellectual qualities. This led to the development of a more nuanced form of palmistry that incorporated the individual's free will and personal responsibility.

Mesopotamia: The Dawn of Civilization

Mesopotamia, often considered the cradle of civilization, also has records of palmistry being practiced. Cuneiform tablets have been discovered that outline the basics of the art, suggesting that it was a well-established practice. In Mesopotamia, palmistry was closely linked with astrology, and it was often used for practical purposes like determining the best times for planting crops or going to war.

Modern Interpretations

Today, palmistry has evolved into a blend of its various historical roots, enriched by modern psychological insights. It is practiced worldwide, both as a form of entertainment and a more serious spiritual practice. Scientific research into dermatoglyphics, the study of the patterns of skin ridges on the fingers and palms, has also lent some credibility to the idea that our hands can reveal something about our personalities and predispositions.

The origins of palmistry are as diverse as they are ancient, reflecting humanity's enduring quest to understand the mysteries of life through the lines etched upon our hands. From the Vedic sages of India to the wise philosophers of Greece, from the holistic healers of China to the mystical priests of Egypt, palmistry has been a mirror reflecting the beliefs, hopes, and fears of countless generations. And as it continues to evolve, it remains a fascinating testament to the complexity and interconnectedness of human culture and spirituality.

Palmistry in the Classical Era, The Greek and Roman Influence

The classical era further contributed to the development of palmistry. The Greek philosopher Anaxagoras (circa 500–428 BCE) is believed to have written a treatise on the subject, which sadly has not survived to the present day. The renowned physician Hippocrates (circa 460–370 BCE) also studied the hands' lines as indicators of a person's health and temperament.

During the Roman era, the scholar Julius Caesar, despite his military pursuits, found interest in the predictive aspects of palmistry. Roman emperor Augustus was also known to have consulted palmists for insights into his fate.

The Middle Ages and Renaissance, Palmistry's Enduring Legacy

Palmistry continued to thrive during the Middle Ages, despite periodic condemnations from the Christian church. During this period, Arabic scholars made significant contributions to palmistry, preserving and expanding the knowledge they had inherited from the ancients. Islamic scholars such as Abu Ali Al-Hasan Ibn Sina (Avicenna) and Abu Ma'shar al-Balkhi were among those who further developed the art of palmistry.

In the Renaissance, a revival of interest in the occult sciences, including palmistry, occurred across Europe. Influential figures such as Paracelsus and Johannes Kepler were known to have practiced and studied palmistry. The publication of books on palmistry, such as "De la physionomie et chiromancie" by Ambroise Paré and "Chiromantia" by Johannes Indagine, further disseminated knowledge about the subject.

Modern Developments, Nellie Simmons Meier and Beyond

The 19th and 20th centuries witnessed a resurgence of palmistry, particularly in Europe and the United States. Notably, the American palmist Nellie Simmons Meier emerged as a trailblazer in the early 20th century. Her pioneering work focused on refining the practice of palmistry by developing systematic approaches to reading the lines and mounts of the hand.

Nellie Simmons Meier's dedication to research, her accurate readings, and her commitment to ethical palmistry solidified her reputation as a respected authority in the field.

Today, palmistry continues to evolve and adapt with the times. While rooted in ancient traditions, modern palmistry integrates scientific, psychological, and intuitive insights to offer a more comprehensive understanding of the human hand and its connection to the individual's personality, potential, and life journey.

As we delve into the depths of palmistry in this book, we honor the ancient wisdom passed down through the ages and celebrate the enduring legacy of Nellie Simmons Meier, whose contributions continue to inspire palmists worldwide. The journey of unlocking the secrets of palmistry begins, inviting us to explore the intricate lines and features that shape our destinies.

CASE STUDY: WALT DISNEY

Walter Elias Disney, born on December 5, 1901, and passing on December 15, 1966, was a renowned American filmmaker, known for his roles as a producer, director, and screenwriter. He is celebrated for his groundbreaking work in animation and for creating the world-famous amusement parks, Disneyland and Disney World. Alongside his brother Roy O. Disney, he established Walt Disney Productions. His creations, including iconic characters like Mickey Mouse and Donald Duck, have become global symbols in various media, from movies to marketing.

Despite his success, Disney's life was marked by personal challenges. He experienced two nervous breakdowns, had a difficult childhood, and faced several film failures. However, he remained undeterred, driven by a mission to provide escapism and joy through his work. His personal life, marked by the sadness of having only one biological child (and one adopted), fueled his passion for creating Disneyland, a testament to his love for his daughters and children everywhere.

Disney's films and theme parks have enchanted millions worldwide, offering a blend of magic, wonder, and happiness. His movies, drawing from fairy tales, children's literature, real-life inspirational stories, and scientific exploration, consistently carried uplifting messages. Disney's legacy is defined by his commitment to family-friendly content, infused with idealism, optimism, and a sense of humor.

Adapted from the notes of Nellie Simmons Meier taken April 14, 1933.

Walt Disney, the visionary behind Mickey Mouse and the Three Little Pigs, had a modest personal style that belied his creative genius. His studio, far from the grandeur of Hollywood, was surprisingly ordinary. Disney's office, reminiscent of a small-town newspaper's, was accessed by a simple wooden staircase leading to a door marked plainly with his name. Inside, the room was functional, filled with a desk, chairs, tables, and an array of drawings and papers.

In this unassuming space, Nellie found Disney deeply immersed in crafting another Mickey Mouse tale. His double-jointed thumbs, a sign of his flair for dramatic storytelling, were busy at work. His square, firm palms suggested a practical, determined nature, balancing his creative spirit with a strong work ethic. Disney's flexible approach to life was evident in his ability to adapt to various people and situations.

For Disney, elaborate surroundings were unnecessary. His focus was solely on his work and its inherent drama. His fingers, though short, indicating a general aversion to minutiae, were uniquely suited to his craft. The long nail phalanges on his third fingers demonstrated a keen eye for line and form, essential in animation. His practicality was further evidenced by the square tips of his fingers.

Disney's hand revealed a high Mount of the Moon, indicative of a vibrant, original imagination and intuitive genius. This trait served as a wellspring of joy and creativity in his work. Despite his natural inclination to avoid details, the length and shape of his fingers, particularly the Saturn finger, underscored his prudence and thoughtful approach, crucial to his success. His long first finger pointed to strong leadership and initiative.

The proportions of his third finger highlighted Disney's affinity for structure and technique, preferring black and white as his artistic medium. His unusually long fourth finger suggested diplomatic skill and a talent for managing his affairs with tact. The length of this finger, along with the long nail phalanges across his hands, reflected his conscientious nature, earning him the complete trust of those he worked with.

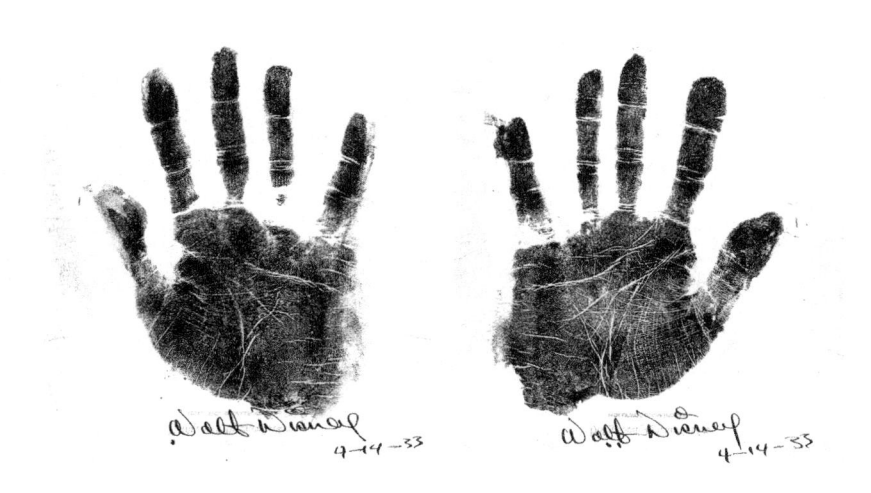

CHAPTER 2

The Basics of Palmistry

In this chapter, we will embark on the first steps of our journey into the art and science of reading palms. Whether you are a curious beginner or an aspiring palmistry practitioner, this chapter will serve as your essential guide to understanding the basics of palmistry and how to approach the study of the human hand.

Palmistry, a practice rich in history and intrigue, stands at the crossroads of art and science. This ancient form of divination, also known as chiromancy, involves reading the lines, shapes, and features of the hands to glean insights into an individual's character and potential future. While it requires dedication to master, even a basic understanding of palmistry can open a window into one's personality and life journey. It's important to approach palmistry with an open mind and a spirit of exploration, as it offers a unique perspective on the human experience.

The Art and Science of Palmistry

Palmistry is often seen as an art due to its interpretive nature. The palmist must be intuitive and sensitive to the nuances of each hand they read, understanding that each line, mound, and finger shape can vary significantly from person to person. This artistic aspect is what makes palmistry so personal and reflective of the individual.

Simultaneously, palmistry is grounded in a form of science. It involves a systematic approach to reading the hands, with specific lines and features having distinct meanings. The practice also draws upon knowledge from various fields such as psychology, anatomy, and even genetics to some extent, as certain hand features can be inherited.

In this Book we will Delve into the Essentials of Palmistry

We began by defining the ancient art of palmistry and its significance in various cultures throughout history. Now we'll move on to discover the fundamental principles that underpin palmistry and understand how the lines, mounts, and features of the hand offer unique insights into an individual's personality, potential, and life journey.

Palmistry, also known as palm reading, is an ancient practice that involves interpreting the lines, shapes, and features of the hand to gain insights into a person's character and future. This fascinating art has intrigued people for centuries, with roots tracing back to various cultures including Indian, Chinese, and Egyptian civilizations.

1. Understanding the Hand Types

Palmistry begins with recognizing the four basic hand types, each associated with different elements and personality traits:

- **Earth Hands:** Characterized by broad, square palms and fingers, thick or rough skin, and a ruddy color. People with earth hands are practical, responsible, and grounded.

- **Air Hands:** Featuring square or rectangular palms with long fingers, often accompanied by dry skin. Those with air hands are intellectual, curious, and good communicators.

- **Water Hands:** Identified by long, oval-shaped palms and long, flexible fingers. Water hand individuals are emotional, sensitive, and creative.

- **Fire Hands:** Distinguished by a square or rectangular palm, but with shorter fingers. People with fire hands are known to be passionate, confident, and industrious.

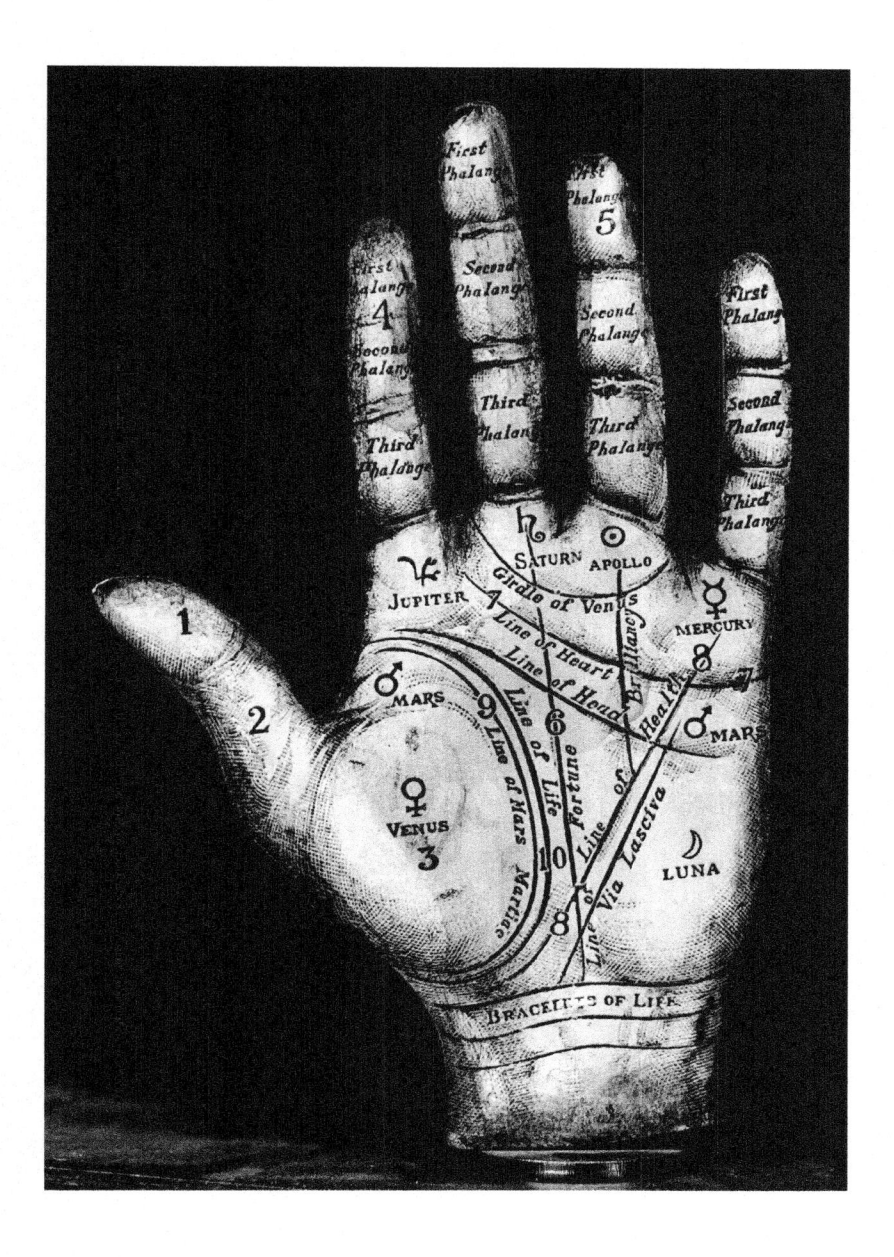

2. Deciphering the Major Lines

The palm houses three major lines, each representing different aspects of life.

The Heart Line: Runs horizontally across the upper part of the palm, reflecting emotional stability, romantic perspectives, and cardiac health.

The Head Line: Found below the heart line, it represents communication style, intellectualism, and knowledge.

The Life Line: Curves around the base of the thumb, indicating vitality, general well-being, and major life changes.

The Fate Line: Also known as the line of destiny, it indicates the degree to which a person's life is affected by external circumstances beyond their control, typically runs vertically from the base of the palm towards the middle of the palm, often ending near or at the base of the middle finger. However, its starting point can vary: it might begin near the wrist, at the Mount of the Moon, or even in the middle of the palm.

3. Examining the Minor Lines

In addition to the major lines, several minor lines can offer more detailed insights:

The Sun Line: Reflects fame, luck, wealth, or scandal.

The Mercury Line: Often linked to health and communication abilities.

The Marriage Lines: Relationships and unions

Other minor lines and their significance

4. Analyzing Mounts and Fingers

The mounts, or raised pads of flesh, on the palm are named after planets and correspond to different personality traits. For example, the Mount of Venus near the thumb relates to love and sensuality, while the Mount of Jupiter under the index finger signifies ambition and leadership.

Fingers and their shapes, lengths, and the prominence of knuckles or nails also hold significance in palm reading, offering further clues about a person's temperament and past experiences.

5. The Role of Hand Dominance

In palmistry, the dominant hand (the one used for writing) represents the current and future life, while the non-dominant hand shows past life or potential.

In palmistry, the dominant and non-dominant hands are believed to hold different meanings, and there are also traditional interpretations that vary between male and female hands.

Dominant vs. Non-Dominant Hand in Palmistry

1. Dominant Hand (Active Hand)

- The dominant hand, usually the one you write with, is considered the "active hand" in palmistry.
- It is believed to represent the present, the active aspects of your life, and the conscious mind.
- The lines, shapes, and features of the dominant hand are thought to show the outcomes of how you have dealt with what life has given you.

2. Non-Dominant Hand (Passive Hand)

- The non-dominant hand is often referred to as the "passive hand."
- It is thought to represent your potential, the subconscious mind, and the traits you were born with.
- This hand is believed to show inherited characteristics and potential, and it may reveal the raw, undeveloped traits of your personality.

Gender Differences in Palmistry:

In traditional palmistry, there used to be a distinction made between male and female hands

- **For Men:** The dominant hand (usually the right if they are right-handed) was read for their external life, such as career and public life. The non-dominant hand was read for the personal and emotional aspects of their life.

- **For Women:** This was traditionally reversed. The non-dominant hand was read for their external life, and the dominant hand for their personal life.

However, these gender-based interpretations are considered outdated by many modern palmists. Contemporary palmistry tends to focus more on the individual, regardless of gender, and interprets the hands based on their dominant and non-dominant status rather than strictly adhering to gender norms.

It's important to remember that palmistry, like any form of divination or personality analysis, is a subjective practice and can vary greatly between practitioners. The interpretations are not scientifically proven and should be taken with a grain of curiosity and open-mindedness.

6. Deciphering the Lines on the Wrist in Palmistry

In the world of palmistry, much attention is given to the lines on the palms and the shape of the hands and fingers. However, the lines on the wrist, also known as bracelet lines or Rascette lines, hold significant meaning as well. These horizontal lines at the base of the palm can provide insights into a person's health, wealth, and longevity. This book delves into the fascinating aspects of these often-overlooked lines in palmistry.

7. Understanding the Bracelet Lines

Typically, most people have two to three visible bracelet lines encircling their wrist. Each line is believed to represent a different aspect of one's life:

- **The First Line:** The line closest to the palm, also known as the health line, is often used to gauge a person's overall well-being and physical health. A clear and unbroken first line suggests good health and physical vitality. If this line is faint or broken, it may indicate health issues or a lack of energy.

- **The Second Line:** This line is associated with wealth, prosperity, and happiness in a person's life. A prominent and unbroken second line is seen as an indicator of financial success and a life of comfort. If this line is fragmented or poorly formed, it might suggest financial struggles or dissatisfaction with life's material aspects.

- **The Third Line:** Not everyone has a third line, but those who do are considered fortunate. This line is linked to influence and fame. A clear third line suggests a person may achieve a status of significance in their life, whether through their career, social status, or personal achievements.

Additional Wrist Lines and Their Meanings

In some cases, individuals may have a fourth or even a fifth line. These are less common and are interpreted as follows:

- **The Fourth Line:** Often seen as an indicator of longevity, a strong fourth line may suggest a long and fulfilling life. This line is also sometimes associated with a strong sense of legacy and leaving a lasting impact on the world.

- **The Fifth Line:** Extremely rare, a fifth line is said to represent certain fame, wealth, and remarkable achievements. It's considered a sign of a life that will be remembered and celebrated.

The Quality of the Lines

The clarity, depth, and continuity of the bracelet lines also play a crucial role in their interpretation. Deep and clear lines are generally seen as positive indicators, while broken, faint, or chained lines might suggest challenges or obstacles in the areas they represent.

Variations in Different Hands

It's important to compare the bracelet lines on both wrists, as variations can provide further insights. For instance, differences in the lines between the dominant and non-dominant hand could indicate changes in lifestyle, health, or fortune over time.

The lines on the wrist in palmistry offer a unique and often overlooked perspective on a person's life journey. While they provide intriguing insights, it's important to remember that palmistry is a subjective art. The interpretations of the bracelet lines, like all aspects of palmistry, should be taken as guidance rather than definitive predictions. As with any form of divination or personality analysis, they offer a lens through which to view potential paths and outcomes, encouraging introspection and self-understanding.

Palmistry is a complex and nuanced practice that offers a unique blend of art and science. While it requires careful study and practice, understanding its basics can provide intriguing insights into one's personality and life path. Remember, palmistry, like any other form of divination, should be approached with an open mind and a sense of exploration.

CASE STUDY: LOWELL THOMAS

Lowell Thomas, an influential American broadcaster and writer, was born on April 6, 1892, in Woodington, Ohio, and passed away on August 29, 1981, in Pawling, New York. He gained fame for his connection with T.E. Lawrence, also known as "Lawrence of Arabia."

In his twenties, Thomas became a war reporter in Europe and the Middle East. His coverage of the Arabian Desert rebellion, particularly his time with Lawrence, played a significant role in popularizing Lawrence. Before he turned 30, Thomas led two expeditions to the Arctic, enhancing his image as a daring journalist.

Thomas's career in broadcasting began at KDKA, a trailblazing radio station in Pittsburgh, in 1926. He moved to CBS in 1930, becoming a renowned radio news commentator. He revisited his war correspondent role during World War II. He was a pioneer in television broadcasting as well, participating in the first TV news broadcast in 1939 and a daily TV program in 1940. He also covered several political conventions for CBS in the 1950s and 1960s. His TV series "High Adventure with Lowell Thomas" (1957–58 on CBS) explored exotic cultures, reminiscent of his earlier lecture tours. Thomas was most famous for his radio broadcasts, which were a staple for American listeners for decades. His signature closing line, "So long, until tomorrow!" also became the title of his 1977 autobiography. Thomas authored over 50 books, including notable works like "With Lawrence in Arabia" (1924) and "The Seven Wonders of the World" (1956).

In her book Lions' Paws, Nellie Simmons Meier makes an example of the hands of Lowell Thomas. This explanation is adapted from her notes.

The intricate lines and mounts on Lowell Thomas's hands, along with the distinct names of the finger joints, are a fascinating study in themselves. Before we delve into a detailed analysis, it's important to first observe these features objectively.

Notice the distinct markings on the fingers. The joints divide each finger into three parts, known as "phalanges": the first or nail phalange, the middle phalange between the first and second joints, and the third phalange near the palm. The form and length of the fingers reveal broad personality traits. For instance, individuals with short, smooth fingers tend to quickly understand overall concepts and often show impatience with minutiae. Conversely, those with knotted short fingers are meticulous and demand thorough evidence before accepting general statements or conclusions.

The traits indicated by the fingers can vary depending on the length of all fingers or a single finger, as well as the shape of their tips. Therefore, it's more accurate to analyze each finger individually. It's uncommon to find hands where all fingers share the same shape or type.

A person with a pointed or tapering first finger is typically quick to understand new concepts and open to fresh ideas.

If the second finger has a moderately pointed tip, it suggests an optimistic nature, with a tendency to see the positive aspects of the present and a hopeful outlook for the future. An extremely pointed tip on this finger, however, may indicate a person who tends to take life lightly, possibly being frivolous or prone to gossip, and often shirking responsibility. Such individuals usually don't dwell on sorrows, preferring to avoid worries and quickly forget unpleasant experiences. Despite this, they can be delightful company, always able to find and bask in the slightest ray of happiness.

A pointed third finger signifies a strong connection to life's beauty. Those who have this feature often cherish the idealistic aspects of life or art, valuing fine details over grand concepts or profound depth.

A person with a pointed fourth finger is typically quick-thinking and has a talent for language. They excel in witty exchanges and can be quite eloquent when the occasion calls for it.

Individuals with square-tipped fingers exhibit distinct characteristics. A square-tipped first finger suggests a person who is cautious about embracing new ideas; they need convincing evidence and time to ponder over things. Such individuals prefer following established paths rather than pioneering new ones. If the second finger is square-tipped, it indicates an individual who appreciates life's joys while being acutely aware of its challenges. A square tip on the third finger points to a pragmatic person, uninterested in fleeting trends or whims. Someone with a square-tipped little finger is adept at presenting well-informed arguments, and if the finger is short, they are likely more effective in written communication than in verbal.

The spatulate fingertip, characterized by a square tip that widens at the sides, represents another distinct group of personalities.

Spatulate tips on the first finger are rare but notable. Individuals with this feature often have extreme views and actions. They can be seen in religious zealots and are known to use unconventional methods in business or other pursuits, sometimes leading to their downfall.

A spatulate second finger indicates a person who is both physically and mentally dynamic, always ready to explore and innovate. This trait is common in explorers, inventors, and researchers who delve into the mysteries of the universe.

Having a spatulate third finger signifies a person with a strong sense of individuality, particularly in creative fields. They are doers, not just dreamers. Their work, whether in art, acting, oratory, or music, is distinctively influenced by their unique personality. For instance, an artist's work is recognizable even without a signature, an actor or orator employs an inimitable technique, and a musician personalizes compositions in their renditions, making them distinctly their own.

A person with a spatulate fourth finger tip is typically dynamic and quick to act, often showing a propensity for explosive speech and actions. When this feature is combined with a spatulate second finger tip, especially in someone engaged in scientific research, it can lead to significant achievements and recognition in the field of discovery.

Turning our attention to Lowell Thomas's hands, we can begin to interpret his fingers. In a comprehensive analysis, these finger tips would be considered in relation to the lines and mounts of the hand, as well as their interrelations. However, even with the basic information provided, we can discern certain aspects about Mr. Thomas.

Overall, his fingers were shorter than his palm, indicating a practical nature. His relatively short first finger suggests a reluctance to take on leadership roles; he had the ability but may have lacked the emotional inclination for such responsibilities. The long nail phalanges across his fingers imply that if he felt obligated to assume a leadership role, his sense of duty would drive him to do so. His quick thinking and action, as indicated by the wide gap between his third and fourth fingers, combined with the diplomatic skills suggested by the length of his little finger and its pointed tip, equipped him to effectively communicate and implement his ideas.

Examining each finger individually, the somewhat square tip of his first finger indicates that Mr. Thomas was open to suggestions but prefered to deliberate before acting.

His second finger, with a slightly spatulate tip, shows his curiosity about the unknown and his willingness to take risks to acquire new knowledge.

The square tip of his third finger reveals a preference for the practical aspects of artistic creations over their mystical or metaphysical elements. He would have sought logical explanations for the existence of various forms of creative art. His interest lay more in functional beauty, such as in architecture, engineering, or shipbuilding, rather than in abstract modern art, which he might have found ambiguous. For Mr. Thomas, music was about rhythm and melody, not abstract musical interpretations of practical themes.

Lastly, the square tip of his fourth finger indicates a preference for prepared speech over impromptu speaking. He would perform better when he had written his speeches beforehand and was committed to conveying the truth as he understood it.

The handprints presented illustrate the lines and mounts on Mr. Thomas's hands. To enhance clarity, the mounts are indicated on the right hand and the lines on the left. It's important to remember that these are merely impressions, mirroring the actual hands, so the right hand appears on the left side and the left hand on the right. In palmistry, the left hand of a person who is predominantly right-handed reveals inherent traits, while the right hand indicates traits that have been acquired or developed. This is reversed for someone who is predominantly left-handed, with the right hand showing inherent traits and the left hand the acquired ones.

When observing the right hand, you'll notice seven distinct mounts, each labeled with their respective names. Below the first finger lies the mount of Jupiter, followed by Saturn under the second finger, Apollo under the third, and Mercury under the fourth. The mount of Venus corresponds to the thumb's third phalanx. Situated across the palm is the mount of the Moon, and positioned above it is the seventh mount, known as upper Mars.

If these mounts or pads are prominent, meaning they are full and rounded, or conversely underdeveloped, appearing flat and almost indented, they reveal certain truths about their owners. However, these indications are always influenced by other features seen in the thumbs, fingers, and lines.

A pronounced mount of Jupiter suggests that the individual is a Jupitarian. With a long finger above this mount, the person tends to be ambitious, possibly a leader, often exuding self-confidence and at times, vanity. Yet, they are invariably warm-hearted. A shorter finger here indicates a lack of initiative and a desire for approval, but a hesitation to take risks to achieve it.

Beneath the second finger lies the mount of Saturn. A well-developed Saturn mount, especially when the second finger is long and the other fingers seem to lean towards it, characterizes a Saturnian. Such individuals often take themselves and others too seriously. A pointed tip on the second finger suggests a more optimistic disposition and a lesser likelihood of remaining single, as strong Saturnians usually shy away from commitments. However, once committed in marriage, they are typically loyal partners. In their professional lives, Saturnians are diligent workers who progress steadily.

The mount of Apollo, located under the third finger, when prominent, indicates a person who is healthy, energetic, versatile, and often exceptionally talented. They have a strong appreciation for beauty and art. The presence of a star on the mount of Apollo, at the end of a line originating from the palm's base, coupled with a long, well-developed third finger that is slightly longer than the second, is a sign of potential genius.

A prominent mount of Mercury, located under the fourth finger, is often found in individuals who are relatively short, have darker complexions, and are characterized by their active nature. These Mercurians are typically restless, both in body and mind, and often exhibit nervous tendencies. They crave variety in their surroundings, experiences, and companions. Mercurians tend to seek partners early in life, usually falling for someone of similar age and disposition.

Male Mercurians are drawn to women who are lively, energetic, and maintain a smart appearance.

In the realm of palmistry, the concept of marriage as a legal or religious bond is not acknowledged. It recognizes emotional connections and passions, but remains indifferent to formal matrimonial ceremonies. A Mercurian values pride in their romantic partner and, if a parent, shows deep devotion to their children.

Mercurians are often creative in discovering ways to generate income. They typically earn money with ease, but without signs of caution in their hands, such as a careful joining of the head and life lines, they may also spend it quickly. They exhibit astuteness, have the ability to motivate others to work for them, and possess considerable diplomatic skills.

The mount at the base of the thumb, known as the mount of Venus, when well-developed, indicates a person likely to have charm, empathy, and gentleness, coupled with a strong attraction to the opposite sex. If the head line is prominent and the thumb rigid, their emotions, while intense, will be under control. However, a pronounced mount of Venus combined with a very pointed second finger is a warning sign: the individual may be capricious, flirtatious, and unreliable in matters of the heart.

The mount of the Moon, situated directly across from the mount of Venus on the palm, signifies imagination and empathy when it is well-developed. The more pronounced this mount is, the stronger these attributes are in the individual.

Another significant mount is that of upper Mars, located just above the mount of the Moon. A prominent upper Mars mount is indicative of bravery and composure, especially in hazardous situations.

Turning our attention back to the hands of Lowell Thomas, we can conduct a more detailed analysis through the lens of these mounts.

The most notable feature on his hands is the mount of the Moon. It bears a unique whorl pattern, akin to a fingerprint. This pattern suggests a kind of intuition, which NSM liked to refer to as a 'sixth sense.' For a writer, this trait infuses their work with a profound sense of human interest; in a singer, it translates to a heartfelt quality in their voice; for a musician, it's often referred to as their exceptional touch. Artists or sculptors with this mark produce work that resonates deeply, much like the sentiments expressed in Richard Realf's poem "Indirection."

> "Back of the canvas that glows
> The painter is hinted and hidden.
> Into the statue that breathes
> The soul of the sculptor is bidden."

In the hands of Lowell Thomas, this characteristic would aptly be termed "personality plus."

His normally developed and firm mount of Venus suggested a strong vitality and vigor. The appeal of its possessor was rooted more in affection, empathy, and a desire to please others, rather than just physical attraction, and he managed this aspect of his personality with care.

The prominent upper mount of Mars highlighted Mr. Thomas's calm demeanor when confronted with danger. Directly beneath this mount was an indication of his serene acceptance of unavoidable circumstances. He was not one to complain or express dissatisfaction. His notable assertiveness was well-balanced by a resilient willpower. He was not one to easily accept defeat, viewing unachieved goals as merely delayed, not forsaken.

The mount located beneath Jupiter, near the first finger, coupled with the finger's length, showed his dedication to hard work, though he showed a preference for collaborative efforts over leadership roles.

The mount of Saturn, and the way the Jupiter and Apollo fingers inclined towards it, indicated that Lowell Thomas had ambition and steadiness, tempered by wise discernment. He was not a typical Saturnian overly serious about life; instead, he approached life with a blend of practicality and rationality.

The elevated mount of Apollo reflected his broad interest in the practical endeavors of others, like inventions and experiments, and also pointed to Mr. Thomas's own diverse creative talents.

The mount of Mercury was notably prominent. Mr. Thomas was distinctly Mercurian, with this mount being the most dominant in his hands. Referring back to the description of a Mercurian, it applies thoroughly to Lowell Thomas. However, there was an exception: the cautious connection between his head and life lines, particularly more pronounced in his right hand than in his left, suggested he consciously exercised restraint, tempering any impulsive tendencies.

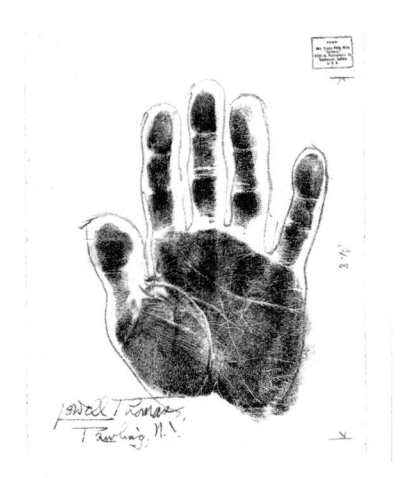

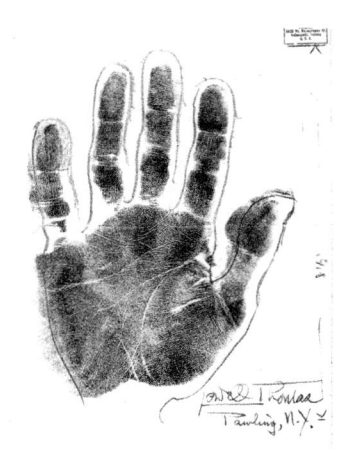

Spatulate Fingers in Palmistry

In palmistry, spatulate fingers refer to a specific finger shape characterized by broad and flared tips that resemble a spatula. This distinct feature is often associated with certain personality traits and tendencies. The appearance of spatulate fingers can vary, but the key characteristic is the widening or flaring of the fingertips, giving them a somewhat spatula-like appearance.

Personality Traits Associated with Spatulate Fingers

1. **Energetic and Active:** Individuals with spatulate fingers are often seen as highly energetic and dynamic. They are typically action-oriented and may have a natural inclination towards physical activities.

2. **Innovative and Creative:** There is a belief that people with spatulate fingers possess a creative and inventive mindset. They are often seen as original thinkers who enjoy exploring new ideas and concepts.

3. **Adventurous and Exploratory:** A love for adventure and exploration is another trait commonly associated with spatulate fingers. These individuals may have a strong desire for travel, new experiences, and unconventional pursuits.

4. **Practical and Resourceful:** People with this finger type are often practical in their approach to life. They are seen as resourceful and capable of finding effective solutions to problems.

5. **Restlessness:** Sometimes, individuals with spatulate fingers might exhibit a degree of restlessness or impatience, always seeking new experiences or challenges.

6. **Independent and Non-conformist:** There is a tendency towards valuing independence and a non-conformist attitude.

People with spatulate fingers may prefer to forge their own path rather than follow traditional routes.

Application in Palmistry

In palmistry, the analysis of finger shapes, including spatulate fingers, is used to complement other aspects of the hand reading, such as the lines on the palm, the shape of the hand, and the length of the fingers. The interpretation can vary depending on the combination of these features and the overall context of the individual's hand.

It's important to remember that palmistry is not a science but a form of divination or a belief system. As such, interpretations like those associated with spatulate fingers are subjective and should be considered more as a source of entertainment or personal reflection rather than definitive or empirical assessments of personality.

CHAPTER 3

The Power of Palm Reading

Unlocking the Secrets of The Hands

Palmistry, or chiromancy, has been a subject of fascination and intrigue for centuries. This ancient practice, which involves studying the lines and features of the hand to interpret personality traits and predict future events, continues to captivate people worldwide.

While skeptics often dismiss palmistry as mere superstition, its enduring appeal lies in its unique blend of art, science, and psychology. This book delves into the power of palmistry, exploring how it offers insights into our lives and why it remains relevant in today's world.

At its core, palmistry is about understanding the self. The human hand, with its intricate lines, shapes, and formations, is seen as a microcosm of the individual. Each line – be it the heart line, head line, life line, or fate line – is believed to tell a story about our emotional well-being, intellectual abilities, life path, and more. The mounts of the hand, named after celestial bodies like Venus, Mars, and Jupiter, are thought to reveal additional aspects of our personality and potential. By interpreting these features, palmists aim to provide a deeper understanding of a person's character, strengths, weaknesses, and potential life experiences.

One of the most compelling aspects of palmistry is its personalized approach. Unlike other forms of divination that rely on external tools or generalized readings, palmistry is based on the unique features of an individual's hand. This personalization makes the practice particularly intimate and reflective, as it encourages introspection and self-awareness. Many people find comfort and guidance in palm readings, as they can offer affirmation, challenge preconceived notions, or provide a new perspective on personal issues.

Palmistry also serves as a bridge between the physical and the metaphysical. It operates on the premise that the physical form is interconnected with the spiritual and emotional realms. This holistic approach resonates with many who seek a deeper understanding of the interconnectedness of their lives. In a world where science and spirituality often seem at odds, palmistry offers a unique space where the two can coexist.

Furthermore, the practice of palmistry fosters a sense of connection and continuity with the past. Originating in ancient India, China, and Egypt, it has been practiced in various cultures for thousands of years. This historical and cultural richness adds to its allure, inviting practitioners and clients alike to be part of a longstanding tradition of human inquiry and mysticism.

In modern times, the relevance of palmistry extends beyond personal readings. It has found a place in therapeutic and counseling settings, where it is used as a tool for self-discovery and personal growth. By providing insights into personality traits and behavioral patterns, palm readings can complement psychological assessments and support personal development goals.

The power of palmistry lies in its ability to offer personal insights, bridge the physical and spiritual realms, and connect us with a rich historical tradition. Whether one approaches it with belief or skepticism, there is no denying the allure of uncovering the secrets held in the palm of our hands. As a tool for reflection, guidance, and self-understanding, palmistry continues to be a fascinating and valuable practice in the quest to understand the complexities of human life.

Getting Started with Palm Reading

Palmistry, the ancient art of interpreting the lines and features of the hand, offers a fascinating window into personality traits and life experiences. For those intrigued by the prospect of understanding life's mysteries through the lines on their palms, getting started in palmistry can be an enriching journey. This beginner's guide aims to provide a foundational understanding of palmistry, offering insights into how to begin this intriguing practice.

Understanding the Basics

Palmistry revolves around the analysis of three primary lines on the palm – the life line, the head line, and the heart line. Each of these lines is believed to represent different aspects of one's life:

1. **The Life Line:** Contrary to popular belief, the life line does not determine the length of your life. Instead, it reflects major life changes, vitality, and physical health.

2. **The Head Line:** This line represents your intellectual tendencies: the way you think, your mental aptitude, and your approach to learning.

3. **The Heart Line:** It indicates emotional aspects, including your relationships, emotional stability, and how you deal with feelings.

The Hands Themselves

In palmistry, both hands are important. The left (or non-dominant) hand is generally believed to represent potential and what you were born with, while the right (or dominant) hand shows what you've done with these qualities. The dominant hand provides insight into your adult life, especially in terms of career and personal achievements.

Mounts and Fingers

Beyond the lines, the mounts (or pads) of the hand and the fingers themselves hold significance. Each mount, named after a planet, represents different attributes. For example, the Mount of Venus (located at the base of the thumb) relates to love and sensuality, while the Mount of Mercury (beneath the pinky finger) relates to communication. The shape, length, and flexibility of the fingers also offer insights into personality traits.

Starting Your Practice

1. **Gather Resources:** Begin with a good palmistry book or online resources that offer detailed explanations of the lines and mounts. Visual aids are particularly helpful in understanding the various aspects of the hand.

2. **Observe Your Hand:** Start by examining your own hands. Take note of the lines' clarity, length, and intersections. Observe the mounts – are they raised or flat? Look at your fingers – are they long, short, straight, or curved?

3. **Practice Regularly:** Like any skill, proficiency in palmistry comes with practice. Start by reading the hands of friends and family. Remember, palmistry is not just about prediction; it's about understanding personality traits and tendencies.

4. **Keep an Open Mind:** Palmistry is a subjective practice. It's important to approach it with an open mind and a sense of exploration. Be aware that interpretations can vary, and much depends on the intuition and experience of the reader.

5. **Join a Community:** Consider joining a palmistry group or online forum. Sharing experiences and insights with others can deepen your understanding and enhance your skills.

6. **Respect Privacy and Sensitivity:** When reading someone else's palms, always approach with respect and sensitivity. Remember that you might be dealing with personal and private aspects of a person's life.

Embarking on the journey of learning palmistry can be deeply rewarding. It offers a unique blend of introspection, art, and psychology. As you begin to unravel the stories told by the lines and features of the hand, you'll gain not just a skill, but a new way of seeing the world and understanding the people in it. Remember, the power of palmistry lies in its ability to offer insights, not definitive answers. With practice and an open heart, the lines on your palm can lead you to a richer understanding of yourself and others.

Tools and Resources for Palmistry Practice

The Role of Hand Analysis Charts

Explore the significance of hand analysis charts, which provide a visual reference for identifying and interpreting the lines, mounts, and other features of the hand. Learn how to use hand analysis charts to enhance your palmistry readings and deepen your understanding of the hand's intricacies.

Books and Literature on Palmistry

Discover the wealth of knowledge available in the form of books, articles, and literature dedicated to palmistry. We will provide a curated list of reputable and influential palmistry resources to guide your further studies and expand your expertise in the field.

Continuing Education and Workshops

Recognize the value of continuous learning and consider attending workshops, seminars, or courses on palmistry to deepen your skills and knowledge. Engaging with experienced practitioners and fellow enthusiasts can offer valuable insights and networking opportunities.

Unraveling Cultural Beliefs in Palmistry

Palmistry's allure transcends borders and cultures, captivating the imagination of people from all walks of life. In this section, we'll explore the widespread belief in palmistry across diverse societies, shedding light on its role in shaping human beliefs, traditions, and rituals. From ancient civilizations to contemporary communities, we discover how palmistry has woven its way into the fabric of human existence, leaving an indelible mark on the human psyche.

The Universality of Palmistry Across Cultures

Palmistry, with its roots deeply embedded in ancient civilizations, has transcended cultural boundaries to become a widely practiced and respected art across the globe. From East to West, North to South, diverse cultures have embraced palmistry as a means to gain insight into human nature, character, and destiny. While each culture may have its unique variations and interpretations, the fundamental belief in the power of palmistry remains a common thread that weaves through the tapestry of humanity.

India: The Vedic Heritage of Hast Samudrik Shastra

As touched on in the last chapter, in India, palmistry is known as "hast samudrik shastra" or "palm samudrik," deeply rooted in Vedic scriptures and ancient wisdom. In Hindu culture, the hands are considered sacred instruments, and the lines etched upon them are believed to be imprints of an individual's past deeds and karmic experiences. Palmistry has been an integral part of Indian society for over five millennia, with esteemed sages and scholars using it to guide and counsel individuals on their life paths.

Indian palmistry incorporates the concepts of the five elements (Earth, Water, Fire, Air, and Ether) and the seven chakras, which influence the lines and features of the hand. Practitioners often combine palmistry with astrology and numerology to provide a more comprehensive analysis of a person's life journey and spiritual evolution.

China: Cheiromancy and the Harmony of Yin and Yang

In China, palmistry is referred to as "cheiromancy" and holds deep roots in ancient Taoist philosophy and traditional Chinese medicine. The hands are considered a microcosm of the human body, and the lines on the palm are believed to reflect the balance of Yin and Yang energies within an individual.

Chinese palmistry places great emphasis on the concept of "wu xing" or the Five Elements (Wood, Fire, Earth, Metal, and Water). Each finger is associated with an element, and the condition of the fingers and lines on the palm is seen as indicative of the person's physical and emotional well-being.

Egypt: Cheirognomy and the Legacy of Ancient Mysteries

In ancient Egypt, palmistry was known as "cheirognomy," where "cheir" means hand, and "gnomon" means to know. The Egyptians regarded the hands as a reflection of the divine order and believed that the lines held hidden knowledge about a person's spiritual and earthly journey.

The Egyptian pharaohs and high priests were known to consult palmists for guidance on important matters, and the art of reading hands was often practiced by the temple priests and scholars. Palmistry's influence in ancient Egypt can be seen in the hieroglyphics and inscriptions that depict pharaohs and dignitaries holding their hands up in symbolic gestures.

Roma (Romani): The Wanderers and Palmistry's Portable Wisdom

The Roma people, often referred to as Romani or Gypsies, have their unique traditions of palmistry that have traveled with them across continents. As nomadic wanderers, the Romani people carried their cultural beliefs, including palmistry, wherever they roamed. Their nomadic lifestyle allowed them to interact with various cultures, and they integrated elements of different palmistry traditions into their own practices.

Roma palmistry, like other cultural variations, places significance on the lines and features of the hand. Their belief in the art is deeply entwined with their storytelling and fortune-telling traditions, adding an enchanting element to their readings.

The Americas, Africa, and Beyond: Diverse Cultural Expressions

Palmistry has also flourished in the Americas, Africa, and other regions, each culture infusing the art with their unique beliefs and practices. Indigenous cultures in the Americas, such as the Native Americans and the Aztecs, have their own interpretations of palmistry, reflecting their spiritual connections with nature and the cosmos.

In Africa, palmistry has been intertwined with various divination practices and spiritual beliefs of different tribes and societies. The interpretation of hand lines and features varies, reflecting the cultural diversity of the continent.

Embracing Diversity, Celebrating Unity

Despite the rich diversity of cultural beliefs in palmistry, a common theme unites them all—the belief that the hands hold a profound story about an individual's life, character, and potential. Whether interpreted through the lens of ancient scriptures, traditional medicine, astrology, or mysticism, palmistry remains a powerful tool for understanding human nature and exploring the mysteries of existence.

As we journey through this comprehensive guide to palmistry, we celebrate the rich tapestry of cultural beliefs that have shaped the art, allowing us to embrace the wisdom and insights from various traditions. Let us continue our exploration, guided by the universal language of the hands, as we unlock the secrets that connect us all in our shared human experience.

Cultural Variations and Symbolism in Palmistry

While the fundamental principles of palmistry resonate across cultures, each society has its unique interpretations and symbolic meanings associated with certain hand features. For instance:

In some cultures, a long and unbroken life line is seen as a sign of longevity and good health, while in others, it may symbolize a stable and predictable life path.

A prominent Apollo (Sun) line may be considered a mark of creativity and artistic talent in one culture, while in another, it may indicate success and recognition in the professional domain.

The shape of the hand itself may hold specific cultural significance. For instance, broad and square hands are often associated with practicality and pragmatism, while long and slender hands may be seen as more sensitive and intuitive.

The presence of specific symbols or markings on the hand may hold unique interpretations across cultures. These symbols can include stars, crosses, triangles, and other shapes that are believed to reveal additional insights about the individual.

Integrating Modern Perspectives and Global Exchange

In the modern era, with the ease of global communication and cultural exchange, palmistry has evolved to embrace a more eclectic approach. Practitioners now have access to diverse cultural beliefs and practices, allowing them to integrate various perspectives into their readings. This cross-cultural pollination enriches the practice of palmistry, providing practitioners with a broader understanding of human nature and the intricacies of the human hand.

Moreover, modern palmistry has also been influenced by advancements in psychology, neuroscience, and other scientific disciplines. The study of personality traits, emotional intelligence, and brain function has led to a deeper appreciation for the connections between the physicality of the hand and the psychological aspects of human behavior.

Universal Themes: The Human Experience in Palmistry

Despite the multitude of cultural variations in palmistry, certain universal themes and principles remain constant. The hands are regarded as a canvas upon which the unique story of an individual's life is imprinted. The lines, mounts, and marks on the hand offer glimpses into one's character, emotions, ambitions, and relationships.

At its core, palmistry transcends cultural barriers to provide individuals with a means of self-awareness and empowerment.

It enables people to gain insights into their strengths, challenges, and potential, thereby helping them make informed decisions and navigate life's complexities with greater understanding.

A Shared Journey of Discovery

As we embark on the journey of unlocking the secrets of palmistry in this comprehensive guide, we celebrate the universal belief in the power of the hands and their potential to reveal the mysteries of the human soul. It is a journey that transcends time, culture, and geography—a journey that connects us all in our shared humanity.

Whether you are an aspiring palmistry practitioner, a curious enthusiast, or simply seeking to delve deeper into the art of self-discovery, this guide aims to be your guiding light. By embracing the wisdom and insights from diverse cultures and traditions, we seek to foster a deeper appreciation for the rich tapestry of human experiences reflected in the lines of our hands.

So, let us continue on this path of exploration, as we peel back the layers of the human hand, and discover the profound truths that lie within. Together, we embark on a journey that unites us in our shared quest for understanding and self-awareness through the universal language of palmistry.

Dispelling Myths and Misconceptions

Throughout history, palmistry has faced skepticism and unwarranted skepticism, leading to numerous myths and misconceptions. We unravel these falsehoods, dispelling common misunderstandings and superstitious notions surrounding palmistry. Armed with accurate information and a deeper understanding of the practice, you will emerge with newfound confidence in exploring the profound insights offered by the lines of the hand.

The journey we are about to embark on is an exploration of both the art and science of palmistry. It is a journey that transcends time, revealing the timeless truths held within the lines and features of the hand. As we delve into each chapter, you will find a wealth of knowledge, practical techniques, and illustrative case studies that will empower you to unlock the secrets held within the palms of yourself and others.

Whether you are a curious enthusiast, a spiritual seeker, or an aspiring professional palmist, "Unlocking the Secrets of Palmistry" aims to be your guiding companion on this path of discovery. So, let us embark on this journey together and open our minds and hearts to the profound wisdom that lies within the ancient art of palmistry.

Palmistry as a Science and an Art

Palmistry, like many ancient practices, has been subject to numerous myths and misconceptions over the centuries. One of the most prevalent misconceptions is the notion that palmistry is solely a mystical or superstitious endeavor. However, modern palmistry incorporates scientific principles, psychology, and statistical analysis, making it a fascinating blend of both science and art.

While the lines and features on the hand are undoubtedly intriguing, palmistry is not meant to predict the future with absolute certainty. Instead, it offers valuable insights into an individual's personality, strengths, challenges, and potential life paths. It is a tool for self-awareness and empowerment, encouraging individuals to take charge of their lives and make informed choices.

The Fixed Destiny Fallacy

Perhaps one of the most significant myths surrounding palmistry is the belief that the lines on the hand dictate an individual's fixed destiny. This misconception assumes that our lives are predetermined and unchangeable. However, palmistry acknowledges the role of free will in shaping our destinies.

While the lines on the hand may provide clues about potential life events and personality traits, they do not determine a person's actions or choices. Palmistry emphasizes that individuals have the power to make decisions and influence the course of their lives through their actions, beliefs, and attitudes.

Hand Size and Fortune

Another common myth is the belief that the size of the hand directly correlates with an individual's wealth or social status. Some people mistakenly think that large hands signify financial success, while small hands suggest poverty. In reality, hand size varies among individuals due to genetic factors and does not hold any inherent connection to one's prosperity or social standing.

Hand size in palmistry is more about relative proportions and the significance of certain hand features, rather than being indicative of material wealth. Palmists focus on analyzing the lines, mounts, and fingers to gain deeper insights into a person's nature and potential.

Only Psychics Can Practice Palmistry

Palmistry is often associated with fortune-telling and psychic abilities, leading to the belief that only individuals with special psychic powers can read palms. However, while intuition can be a valuable asset in palmistry, it is not the sole requirement for accurate readings.

Palmistry is a skill that can be learned, practiced, and honed through study and experience. While some practitioners may have a natural affinity for understanding the nuances of hand features, the art of palmistry can be mastered by anyone willing to invest time and dedication into learning the various elements of hand analysis.

Negative Stereotypes and Stigma

Throughout history, palmistry has been subjected to negative stereotypes and stigmatization, often associating it with superstition, charlatanism, and unethical practices. These stereotypes have been perpetuated through fictional portrayals in literature, movies, and popular culture, further fueling misconceptions about palmistry.

However, it is essential to separate fact from fiction and recognize that reputable palmists uphold ethical principles, emphasizing the value of empowering individuals rather than exploiting their fears or vulnerabilities. Ethical palmists prioritize consent, confidentiality, and a non-judgmental approach in their practice.

The Value of Self-Discovery and Reflection

Dispelling myths and misconceptions surrounding palmistry allows us to embrace its true value as a tool for self-discovery and introspection. Palmistry offers a unique and holistic way to understand ourselves and others, promoting self-awareness, empathy, and personal growth.

As we explore the intricate lines and features of the hand, let us approach palmistry with an open mind and a willingness to delve into the rich symbolism and wisdom it offers. By dispelling the myths that obscure its true essence, we can truly appreciate the art of palmistry as a powerful means of understanding the human experience and embracing the complexities of our unique life journeys. Let us embark on this enlightening journey together, as we uncover the profound insights held within the lines of the human hand.

The Role of Skepticism and Critical Thinking

Healthy skepticism and critical thinking are essential when exploring any form of divination, including palmistry. While palmistry has a long history and is embraced by many cultures, it is essential to approach it with a balanced perspective. Embracing a skeptical outlook can help individuals discern between genuine practitioners who adhere to ethical standards and those who may exploit others' vulnerability.

A critical approach allows us to evaluate palmistry based on evidence, logical reasoning, and practical applications. By seeking out reputable sources, studying scientific research related to hand analysis, and engaging with knowledgeable practitioners, individuals can gain a deeper appreciation for the legitimacy and value of palmistry as a means of self-exploration.

Recognizing the Subjectivity of Interpretation

An important aspect of palmistry to acknowledge is that interpretations may vary among practitioners. While there are fundamental principles and traditional meanings associated with hand features, the art of palmistry also allows for subjective insights based on the individual reader's intuition and expertise.

Interpreting the lines and features of the hand is an intricate process that requires careful consideration of the overall context. The practitioner takes into account the hand's shape, size, finger proportions, and the interplay between different lines and mounts. Additionally, a skilled palmist considers the individual's background, personality, and life experiences to offer a more accurate reading.

Ethical Considerations in Palmistry Practice

As with any form of divination or counseling, ethical considerations are of utmost importance in palmistry. Ethical palmistry practitioners prioritize the well-being of their clients and respect their right to privacy and personal agency. They do not make extreme or alarming predictions that may cause unnecessary distress or anxiety.

Ethical palmists also avoid exploiting vulnerable individuals or manipulating them for personal gain. They present the information in a compassionate and constructive manner, encouraging clients to view the insights gained from palmistry as tools for growth and self-improvement.

Empowerment through Self-Knowledge

Beyond the myths and misconceptions, the heart of palmistry lies in its ability to empower individuals to gain a deeper understanding of themselves and their life paths. Through palmistry, individuals can recognize their inherent strengths, confront challenges, and make informed decisions that align with their values and aspirations.

Palmistry encourages self-reflection and introspection, enabling individuals to gain insights into their emotions, relationships, and career aspirations. Armed with this self-knowledge, individuals can navigate life's complexities with increased self-confidence and a greater sense of direction.

Embracing the Art and Science of Palmistry

As we dispel myths and misconceptions surrounding palmistry, we uncover the true essence of this ancient art. It is a dynamic and ever-evolving practice that integrates elements of science, psychology, and intuitive understanding.

By embracing palmistry with an open mind and a willingness to explore its intricacies, we can recognize its value as a powerful tool for self-awareness and personal growth. Whether seeking guidance in career decisions, relationships, or life's challenges, palmistry provides a unique lens through which to gain insights and perspective.

Let us approach the study and practice of palmistry with curiosity, respect, and an appreciation for its diversity and universality. As we delve into the lines and features of the human hand, we embark on a journey of self-discovery and exploration, uncovering the timeless wisdom and profound truths that lie within us all.

Case Studies: Helen Hayes, Maude Adams and Ethel Barrymore

Adapted from the book Lions' Paws

The two most common career questions Nellie said she encountered were, "Can I succeed in acting or writing?" It seemed almost everyone dreamt of becoming an actor or a writer.

In some cases, a person's hands reveal undeniable talent and the mental and physical health to nurture it, and she could confidently predict success in any field they were drawn to. Others have diverse talents that, with hard work and opportunity, can lead to success. Nellie believed that even the greatest achievers may owe their fame to their circumstances as much as to their innate abilities.

Among the notable individuals discussed in this chapter, they share one trait: smooth fingers, at least up to the second joints. This signifies inspirational qualities. They could seize opportunities instinctively, either through visualizing their actions, or by using innate methods.

Consider Helen Hayes, the enchanting actress. In 1921, her stage manager, William Seymour, asked Nellie to read her hands. These hands, with satiny skin and short fingers, indicated a quick, inspirational mind, perfect for her roles. On her Mount of the Moon, a whorl signified a sixth sense, an ability to bring characters to life. Her hands showed hard work and adaptability, with a flexible left thumb and a stiffer right, indicating a mix of willpower and methodical work. Her hands' openness and smooth fingers suggested her talent for shedding unnecessary details and immersing herself in her characters.

If you contrast this with Maude Adams, another gifted actress. When Nellie first read Maude's hands, she was already curious about her potential. Unlike Hayes, Adams' thumbs lacked flexibility, indicating a strong will and stubbornness. This trait was evident in her unwavering interpretation of roles. While Hayes' Mount of Venus showed a balance of head and heart, Adams' was flatter, her interpretations more intellectually imaginative. Both actresses brought unique interpretations to their roles, reflecting their distinct hand characteristics.

James M. Barry, upon seeing Maude Adams perform, instantly knew she was the perfect choice for his character, My Lady Babbie. Her hands, with a line between the heart and headlines, hinted at international recognition, which she indeed achieved.

In the world of acting and writing, success is a blend of innate talent, hard work, and the ability to seize opportunities. As seen in the hands of Hayes and Adams, each person brought their unique qualities to their art.

Helen Hayes, born on October 10, 1900, in Washington, D.C., and passing away on March 17, 1993, in Nyack, New York, was an acclaimed American actress, often hailed as the "First Lady of the American Theatre." Encouraged by her mother, a stage performer, Hayes began her acting journey in her early years, joining the Columbia Players from 1905 to 1909 and making her Broadway debut at age nine in "Old Dutch." She gained popularity in her teen years through roles in productions like "Pollyanna" (1917) and "Dear Brutus" (1918).

Hayes's career took off in 1920 with her role in the comedy "Bab," leading to her starring in the silent film "The Weavers of Life." Her breakthrough came in 1926 with James Barrie's "What Every Woman Knows." In 1928, she married journalist and playwright Charles MacArthur, with whom she remained until his death in 1956.

Transitioning to Hollywood in 1931, Hayes won an Academy Award for "The Sin of Madelon Claudet." Despite further film roles, she preferred the stage, achieving remarkable success in "Mary of Scotland" (1933) and "Victoria Regina" (1935). She won the first Tony Award for best actress for her role in "Happy Birthday" (1946).

Hayes's film career revived with "Airport" (1970), earning her a second Academy Award. She continued acting in films and television into the mid-1980s, including the TV series "The Snoop Sisters" (1973) and as Miss Marple in several TV movies. She authored four autobiographies and was recognized for her acting and humanitarian work, receiving the Presidential Medal of Freedom in 1986. Two Broadway theatres were named in her honor. Her children, Mary and James MacArthur, also pursued acting careers.

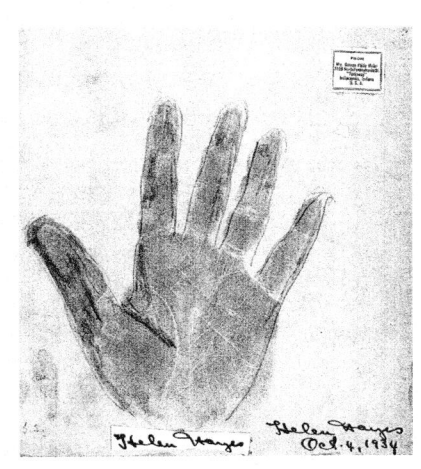

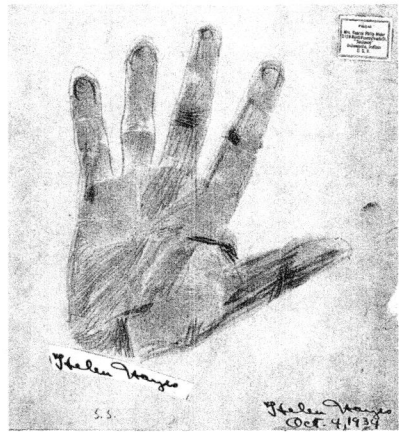

Maude Adams, born November 11, 1872, in Salt Lake City, Utah, and deceased July 17, 1953, in Tannersville, New York, was a celebrated American actress famous for her roles in Sir James Barrie's plays. Starting her acting career at five in San Francisco, she quickly rose to fame, especially after joining E.H. Sothern in 1888 and later partnering with John Drew in 1892 under Charles Frohman's management. Adams became well-known for her performances in "The Little Minister," "Peter Pan," and other notable plays, including several Shakespearean roles. She retired in 1918, briefly experimented with stage lighting, returned to acting in the early 1930s, and ended her stage career in 1934. Adams later taught dramatic art at Stephens College, Missouri, from 1937.

Adapted from the notes of Nellie Simmons taken April 3rd, 1901

When Nellie first encountered Maude Adams in Indianapolis in April 1901, she was performing with John Drew in "Rosemary". Ethel Barrymore was also there, making her post-convent school debut in a minor but captivating role. Adams was charmingly open and eager about having her hands read, showing both enthusiasm and a keen interest in my interpretations.

Adams' thumb, flaring widely from her hand, suggested her generous nature in spending time, effort, and money on others, driven by a strong sense of duty. Her stiff thumb indicated her selective social nature, preferring congenial company and avoiding offense in social settings. This stiffness also highlighted her need for quiet environments for physical and mental recuperation.

Her sloping palm towards the wrist reflected her artistic inclinations. Long, slim fingers pointed to her meticulous attention to detail, while developed middle joints showed her love for order in both material and intellectual realms. The smoothness of her fingers from tips to joints revealed her inspirational approach, tempered by analytical thinking.

Adams' long first finger indicated her leadership and planning skills, with a balanced sense of mercy and justice. Her second finger suggested idealism and a positive outlook on life, while her third finger indicated a preference for structure over color in her artistic tastes. The fourth finger's flare and length denoted quick thinking and diplomatic skills, essential in her professional interactions.

Her nails, shorter and broader, hinted at a critical and introspective nature, which she channeled into understanding the nuances of her characters. Despite a natural mental irritability, she maintained control over her emotions, evident in her thumb type and diplomatic little finger.

There was a notable difference between the lines of her right and left hands. Her left hand showed impulsiveness and optimism, while her right hand demonstrated a more fact-based, tolerant approach, influenced by her intuitive understanding of others' perspectives. Adams was deeply loyal to her loved ones.

The lower mount on her hand's outside bore marks Nellie associated with a 'sixth sense', a trait of creative genius in art. This quality in Adams' hands suggested her ability to convincingly portray her roles, submerging her personality into the characters with a blend of imagination and subtlety.

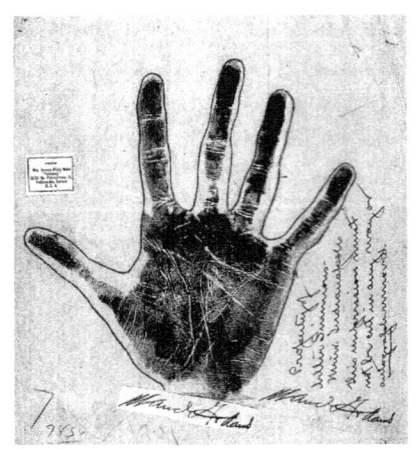

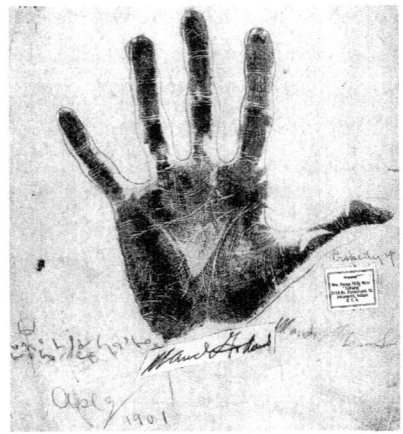

Adapted from the notes of Nellie Simmons taken December, 1908

Ethel Barrymore (1879-1959) was a celebrated American actress and a member of the renowned Barrymore family, a dynasty known for its significant contributions to the stage and screen. Born Ethel Mae Blythe on August 15, 1879, in Philadelphia, Pennsylvania, she was the daughter of actors Maurice Barrymore and Georgiana Drew Barrymore, and the sister of John and Lionel Barrymore, both of whom were also acclaimed actors.

Barrymore's acting career began in the 1890s, and she quickly gained recognition for her talent and charisma. She made her Broadway debut in 1895 and soon became known for her captivating performances in both comedies and dramas. Her stage presence was marked by a unique blend of elegance and emotional depth, which endeared her to audiences and critics alike.

In 1901, Barrymore achieved critical acclaim for her performance in "Captain Jinks of the Horse Marines," which solidified her status as a leading actress on Broadway. Over the next few decades, she starred in numerous successful plays, including "The Second Mrs. Tanqueray," "A Doll's House," and "The Constant Wife." Her performances were characterized by her powerful stage presence and her ability to convey complex emotions with subtlety and grace.

Barrymore also made a significant impact in the early days of cinema, though she always considered the stage her true home. She appeared in several silent films and later transitioned to sound films, delivering memorable performances in movies such as "None but the Lonely Heart" (1944), for which she won an Academy Award for Best Supporting Actress.

Apart from her illustrious acting career, Barrymore was known for her strong personality and her commitment to the arts. She was a respected figure in the theatrical community and was often sought after for her insights and mentorship by emerging actors.

Ethel Barrymore passed away on June 18, 1959, leaving behind a legacy as one of the most distinguished actresses of her time. Her contributions to American theater and film have made her a lasting icon in the entertainment industry, and her name remains synonymous with the golden age of American stage and screen.

When NSM first encountered Ethel Barrymore, she was embarking on her initial professional tour, fresh out of a convent school and playing a minor role alongside Maude Adams and John Drew in "Rosemary." Seven years later, during her performance in "Alice, Sit by the Fire," NSM captured impressions of her hands, revealing their distinct characteristics.

Barrymore's hands were notable for their diverse qualities. The wide spread of her fingers, reminiscent of a starfish, indicated a strong sense of independence in thought and action, bordering on recklessness. Her palms were notably resilient, reflecting a carefree approach to life and a lack of concern for future planning. Her thumbs, with a disproportionately long first phalange, suggested a dominant will that could overshadow reason and logic, turning into stubbornness in the face of even slight opposition.

The long first finger of Jupiter in her hand also pointed to a love of power and a desire to lead, regardless of the consequences. The pointed tip of her thumb highlighted her impatience for results, underlining a restless and impulsive temperament. However, Barrymore's gifts were evident in her beautifully placed, nicely shaped, and highly flexible fingers, showcasing her versatility, mental agility, and ability to master a wide range of emotions in her performances.

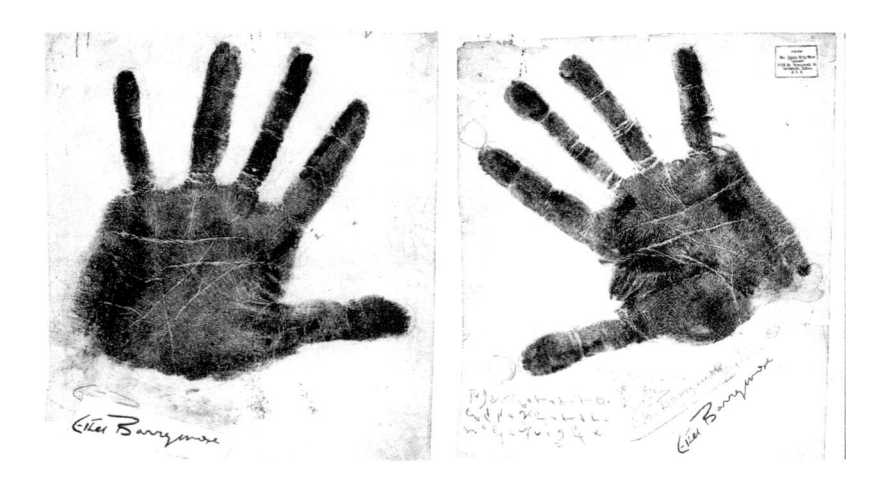

Her relatively short, smooth fingers suggested a distaste for minutiae, balanced by common sense and prudence, as indicated by the length and position of her headline and the second phalange of the finger of Saturn. These traits helped her navigate situations that might have overwhelmed others less determined or talented.

The lines under her third finger further underscored her exceptional abilities. In her left hand, multiple lines of similar clarity and depth suggested that Barrymore could have succeeded in music or writing. The distinct fork of brilliancy in her right hand indicated her wise decision to channel her varied talents into dramatic expression, enhancing her performances with her vocal beauty and instrumental skills. Her keen eye for lines and love of color, as shown in the development of her third finger's nail phalange and the second phalange, were advantageous in planning her costumes and stage sets.

CHAPTER 4

The Four Hand Types

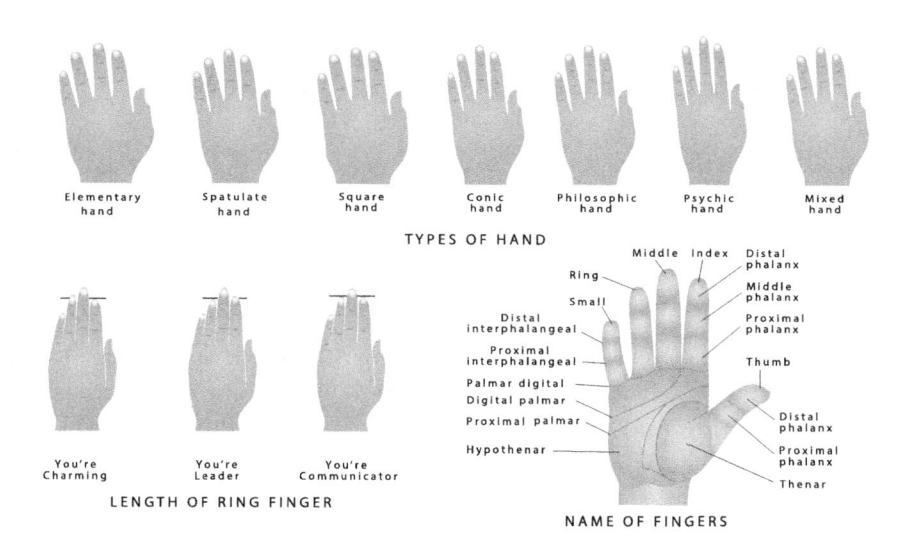

Elementary hand | Spatulate hand | Square hand | Conic hand | Philosophic hand | Psychic hand | Mixed hand

TYPES OF HAND

You're Charming | You're Leader | You're Communicator

LENGTH OF RING FINGER

Middle, Index, Ring, Small — Distal phalanx, Middle phalanx, Proximal phalanx, Distal interphalangeal, Proximal interphalangeal, Palmar digital, Digital palmar, Proximal palmar, Hypothenar, Thumb, Distal phalanx, Proximal phalanx, Thenar

NAME OF FINGERS

The Four Elements in Palmistry

Palmistry, like many other ancient practices, draws inspiration from the concept of the four classical elements: Earth, Water, Fire, and Air. Each of these elements is believed to influence an individual's personality, behavior, and life experiences, and their presence is reflected in the shape, texture, and features of the hand.

The Earth Hand: Stability and Practicality

The Earth hand is characterized by a square-shaped palm with fingers that are proportionate in length. Individuals with Earth hands are often practical, reliable, and grounded in their approach to life. They possess a strong work ethic and are dependable in fulfilling their responsibilities. People with Earth hands are often attuned to the physical world and find comfort in traditional and straightforward methods.

In palmistry, Earth hands are associated with traits such as patience, perseverance, and a deep connection to nature. They often excel in fields that require practical skills and hands-on work, such as agriculture, craftsmanship, and building.

The Water Hand: Sensitivity and Intuition

The Water hand is distinguished by a rectangular palm shape and long, tapering fingers. Individuals with Water hands are known for their emotional depth, sensitivity, and strong intuition. They possess a keen ability to understand the feelings and emotions of others, making them empathetic and compassionate individuals.

People with Water hands are often drawn to creative pursuits and have a natural talent for artistic expression, music, and healing arts. Their intuition guides them in decision-making, and they are attuned to the subtle energies of the world around them.

The Fire Hand: Passion and Energy

The Fire hand is recognizable by its palm shape, which is longer than it is wide, and its short, strong fingers. Those with Fire hands are often characterized by their passionate nature, enthusiasm, and high energy levels. They are ambitious and driven individuals, always seeking new challenges and opportunities.

People with Fire hands are natural leaders and have a strong desire to make a positive impact on the world. They excel in fields that require charisma, motivation, and a competitive spirit. Fire hands are associated with traits such as creativity, assertiveness, and a zest for life.

The Air Hand: Intellect and Communication

The Air hand is typified by a square-shaped palm with long, slender fingers. Individuals with Air hands are known for their analytical minds, quick wit, and excellent communication skills. They possess a love for knowledge and enjoy intellectual pursuits and learning.

People with Air hands are often drawn to fields such as writing, teaching, and research. They have a talent for problem-solving and excel in tasks that require logical thinking and clear communication.

Hand Combinations and Elemental Balance

It is essential to note that while some individuals may exhibit a dominant element in their hands, most people have a combination of different elements, each contributing to their unique personality. The presence of multiple elements in a person's hands can create a balance of traits, making them well-rounded and adaptable individuals.

The interpretation of elemental balance in palmistry involves observing the interplay of hand features, including the shape of the hand, the length and proportions of the fingers, and the prominence of specific lines and mounts. A skilled palmist can identify the dominant elements in a person's hands and provide insights into their strengths, challenges, and potential life paths.

Embracing Elemental Wisdom in Palmistry

Understanding the role of the four elements in palmistry allows practitioners to offer more nuanced and insightful readings. By recognizing the elemental influences present in an individual's hands, palmists can help clients gain a deeper understanding of themselves and their interactions with the world.

As we delve into the intricacies of the four elements in palmistry, we uncover the rich tapestry of human experiences reflected in the lines of the human hand. Embracing elemental wisdom in palmistry enables us to connect with the elemental forces that shape our lives, guiding us towards a more profound understanding of ourselves and our place in the universe. Through the lens of the four elements, let us continue our journey of self-discovery, wisdom, and growth in the art of palmistry.

Unlocking the Elemental Mysteries

We're going on an exciting journey into the heart of human nature in the world of palmistry. Think of your hands as the doorways to your innermost self, opening them to expose stories and secrets that words alone cannot express. Earth, Air, Water, and Fire are the four unique hand kinds introduced as part of the elemental classification of hands. Our compass is this age-old knowledge, which leads us through the complex terrain of character qualities, assets, and weaknesses.

The Hand as a Reflection of Personality

Analyzing Hand Shapes

Dive into the world of hand shapes and their relation to the four classical elements: Earth, Water, Fire, and Air. Discover how hand shapes reveal distinctive personality traits and tendencies.

The Fingers: Windows to the Soul

Explore the role of the fingers in hand analysis, as they provide valuable insights into a person's communication style, thinking patterns, and emotional expression.

Elemental classification - The Hands' Elemental Dance

Earth Hands: Grounded & Practical

Earth hands are associated with realism and grounding in the field of palmistry. The palms of these hands are square, and the fingers are unyielding. People with Earth hands have a strong sense of pragmatism and steadfast dependability. They face life's problems with both feet firmly planted and steadfastly determined. They define dependability and success in professions requiring a strict work ethic.

Air Hands: Intellectual & Expressive

As we move on to Air hands, think of them as the scribes of the human experience. With square or rectangular palms and long, nimble fingers, they symbolize intellectual prowess and expressive eloquence. Air hands invite us into thought, curiosity, and communication. They are the storytellers, educators, and creators who thrive in the realm of ideas.

Water Hands: Intuitive & Emotional

Our journey flows into Water hands, where emotion reigns supreme. Imagine palms with long fingers and soft, sensitive skin, akin to the canvas of a master painter. Water hands are intuitive, empathetic, and deeply connected to the ebb and flow of feelings. They find their calling in artistic endeavors, counseling, and professions that require emotional intelligence.

Fire Hands: Energetic & Ambitious

Finally, Fire hands—the personification of zeal and ambition—ignite our curiosity. Think of palms that are square or rectangular with short fingers and that exude a noticeable vitality. Fire hands are the doers, the sparks of change, and the leaders. They excel in professions that call for zeal and an insatiable drive for success.

Deciphering Your Hand's Tale

The Shape of Your Hand

As we dive deeper into understanding your own hands, consider the shape of your palm. Does it resonate with the solidity of Earth, the expansiveness of Air, the fluidity of Water, or the fiery determination of Fire? This basic characteristic sets the stage for the story your hands wish to tell.

Finger Length and Proportions

Each finger reveals a characteristic of your hand. Pay close attention to the proportions and length of your fingers. Are they consistent with the descriptions of the elements? Each element has special finger characteristics to share: Earth, Air, Water, and Fire.

Texture and Consistency of Your Palm

Your palm's texture is like a painting canvas's texture, adding depth to the narrative. Are your hands coarse and practical like Earth, smooth and intellectual like Air, soft and empathetic like Water, or fiery and energetic like Fire? The texture speaks volumes about your inner self.

Flexibility and Movement

Watch how your hands flex and move. Do your movements have the same weight as Earth? Do you frequently use gestures and express yourself freely, like Air? Your hands may have the grace and emotional resonance of Water, or they may radiate Fire's ferocious force and ambition.

The Role of Thumb and Fingertips

Finally, the narrative of your hand is punctuated by the thumb and fingertips. They highlight your character with distinguishing traits. Does the pragmatism of Earth, the cerebral sophistication of Air, the emotional depth of Water, or the dynamism of Fire align with your thumb and fingertips?

Remember that palmistry is both an art and a science as we reveal the layers of your particular hand type. Your hands serve as a road map to help you navigate the complex terrain of your personality. As we explore the mysteries in your hands, remember to remain interested and kind. You will be able to identify your hand type by the end of this chapter. You will also be able to appreciate the rich tapestry of human variability that is mirrored in these fundamental hands.

Characteristics and Significance of Each Hand Type

Earth Hands: Grounded & Practical

Earth hands are the embodiment of stability and practicality. They anchor individuals to the physical world with square palms and short, sturdy fingers. These hands signify a strong work ethic, dependability, and a no-nonsense approach to life. Earth hand bearers are the rock-solid foundations in both personal and professional spheres.

Significance

Jobs requiring dependability and attention to precision are best suited for earth hands. They are dependable companions, partners, and colleagues you can always count on. They provide stability and a feeling of security in partnerships. The presence of Earth hands implies a down-to-earth, practical outlook on life.

Air Hands: Intellectual & Expressive

The intelligent and communicative members of the hand types are air hands. They represent analytical reasoning and expressive communication with square or rectangular palms and long, slender fingers. These hands represent the capacity to express concepts clearly, a love of ideas, and curiosity.

Significance

Airhands find their calling in professions related to writing, teaching, public speaking, and any field that demands effective communication. They are the storytellers, thinkers, and educators who thrive on exchanging ideas. In personal relationships, they are engaging conversationalists and excellent listeners. The presence of Air hands suggests a natural curiosity and intellectual depth.

Water Hands: Intuitive & Emotional

Water hands are the poets and empaths of the hand types. With long palms and fingers, often with soft and sensitive skin, they are deeply attuned to their emotions and the emotions of others. These hands signify heightened intuition, creativity, and emotional intelligence.

Significance

The arts, psychotherapy, and medical professions are common places where water hands find their calling. They are therapists, artists, and compassionate people who are excellent at emotionally understanding and connecting with others. Interpersonal connections benefit from their sensitivity and in-depth understanding of emotions. Having Water hands denotes a sensitive and imaginative nature.

Fire Hands: Energetic & Ambitious

Fire hands are the dynamos, the movers, and shakers of the hand types. Featuring square or rectangular palms with short fingers, they radiate an infectious energy and a relentless drive for success. These hands signify ambition, passion, and a burning desire to achieve.

Significance

Firehands excel in leadership positions, business ventures, and any endeavor that requires zeal and a can-do mentality. They set an example for others by serving as inspiration, motivators, and change agents. They infuse energy and a daring attitude towards difficulties into interpersonal connections. The presence of Fire hands suggests an energetic and ambitious personality.

Discovering Your Hand's Elemental Essence

As you explore the characteristics and significance of each hand type, you may find resonance with one or a combination of these elemental traits. Your hand type doesn't define you entirely, but it provides valuable insight into your dominant personality traits and tendencies.

Embracing Diversity in Hand Types

Keep in mind that diversity is what makes palmistry so beautiful. These hand types are present in the human population, just as all four elements coexist harmoniously in nature. Some people might only have one dominant hand type, while others might have a combination of two or more. This variety of hand styles reflects the depth and richness of human nature.

The Power of Self-Discovery

Understanding your hand type is ultimately a fantastic self-discovery tool. It enables you to embrace your flaws, capitalize on your strengths, and go through life with greater awareness. Every hand kind, made of Earth, Air, Water, or Fire, has unique abilities to impart. Accept your diversity and that of the world, and let yourself take the reins on this magnificent journey of self-discovery.

How to Identify Your Hand Type

Finding your hand type is fun and provides insightful information about your personality. Understanding your hands' characteristics will help you unravel the mysteries of your inner self. Your hands are like a personal roadmap. Step by step, let's begin this exciting adventure of self-discovery.

1. The Shape of Your Palm: The Foundation

The foundation of identifying your hand type lies in the shape of your palm. Begin by examining the overall shape of your palm. Place your hand flat on a table or hold it to the light. Your palm can fall into one of these four categories:

- **Square Palm (Earth):** If your palm appears square, with the length roughly equal to the width, you may have Earth hands. These hands suggest a practical and grounded personality.

- **Rectangular Palm (Air):** A rectangular palm, with a longer length than the width, might indicate Air hands. This shape signifies intellectual curiosity and effective communication skills.

- **Long Palm (Water):** If your palm is long, with fingers that seem to extend elegantly from the wrist, you could have Water hands. These hands are associated with emotional depth and intuition.

- **Square with Short Fingers (Fire):** A palm that appears square, with shorter fingers, could signify Fire hands. These hands radiate ambition and energy.

2. Finger Length: The Fine Print

After determining your palm shape, turn your attention to your fingers. The length of your fingers concerning your palm can provide additional clues to your hand type. Here's what to look for:

- **Earth Hands:** Earth hands typically have shorter fingers than the palm size. These fingers suggest practicality and a no-nonsense approach to life.

- **Air Hands:** Air hands feature longer, more graceful fingers extending beyond the palm's base. These fingers highlight intellectual finesse and effective communication.

- **Water Hands:** Water hands have long fingers with a graceful taper, giving the hand an artistic and sensitive appearance. This trait indicates emotional depth and intuition.

- **Fire Hands:** Fire hands are characterized by short fingers that seem sturdy and powerful. These fingers symbolize ambition and a dynamic approach to life.

3. Texture and Consistency: The Canvas

The texture of your palm's skin is like the canvas on which your hand's story is written. Run your fingers over your palm and pay attention to the texture and consistency:

- **Earth Hands:** If your palm's skin feels coarse and practical, reminiscent of a well-used tool, you may have Earth hands. This texture reflects a grounded, down-to-earth nature.

- **Air Hands:** Air hands often have smooth and fine-textured skin. The softness suggests intellectual depth and a refined quality.

- **Water Hands:** Water hands are characterized by soft and sensitive skin. Running your fingers over them feels like caressing a delicate surface. This texture aligns with their emotional depth and empathy.

- **Fire Hands:** Fire hands tend to have firm and coarse skin. When you touch them, it's like feeling the energy and ambition within. This texture mirrors their dynamic and ambitious nature.

4. Flexibility and Movement: The Flow

Watch how your hands flex and move. These movements can reveal further details about your hand type:

- **Earth Hands:** Earth hands frequently move firmly and with a sense of purpose. Their purposeful motion frequently reflects useful acts.

- **Air Hands:** Air hands have an elegant, expressive gait similar to a director leading an orchestra. These hands tend to make expressive motions.

- **Water Hands:** The soft, flowing motion of water hands is comparable to the calming beat of Water. Their motions are frequently smooth and emotionally impactful.

- **Fire Hands:** Fire hands move with vigor and purpose, displaying dynamic, energizing gestures. These hands are always moving, which is indicative of their ambitious attitude.

5. The Role of Thumb and Fingertips: The Details

Lastly, focus on the thumb and fingertips, as these details add nuance to your hand type:

- **Earth Hands:** The thumb on Earth hands is usually sturdy and functional. The fingertips' squared-off or blunt edges highlight their grounded nature.

- **Air Hands:** Long, elegant thumbs are a common feature of air hands. The fingertips are elegant and tapered, reflecting their intellectual finesse.

- **Water Hands:** Water hands have thumbs with a soft, rounded appearance. Their fingertips are sensitive and finely shaped, echoing their emotional depth.

- **Fire Hands:** Fire hands possess thumbs that are short and powerful. The fingertips may be square, underlining their dynamic energy and ambition.

Embrace Your Unique Hand Type

Remember that palmistry is not about strict definitions but rather the individual tapestry of your personality as you piece together the qualities of your hand. One hand type may be the one with which you most strongly identify, or you may exhibit qualities from several other types. Accept yourself for who you are, and allow your handwriting to guide you as you explore who you are.

Unlocking the Secrets of Hand Analysis

Now that you've identified your hand type, the next step is to delve deeper into the fascinating world of interpreting your hand's lines, mounts, and features. These elements will provide even more profound insights into your life's journey.

Hand Shapes and Types

In palmistry, the study of hand shapes and types is a foundational aspect of analyzing the human hand. The shape of the hand provides valuable insights into an individual's personality, character traits, and tendencies. Each hand shape is associated with distinct characteristics, and understanding these shapes helps palmists offer more accurate and comprehensive readings.

The Earth Hand: Stability and Practicality

The Earth hand is distinguished by its square-shaped palm and fingers that are proportional in length. Individuals with Earth hands are practical, reliable, and grounded in their approach to life. They are often known for their strong work ethic and the ability to diligently fulfill their responsibilities. People with Earth hands are down-to-earth and prefer straightforward and traditional methods.

In palmistry, the Earth hand is associated with qualities such as patience, endurance, and a deep connection to nature. These individuals find comfort in physical activities and often excel in practical fields such as agriculture, craftsmanship, and building. They are trustworthy friends and family members, often providing stability and support in their relationships.

The Water Hand: Sensitivity and Intuition

The Water hand is recognized by its rectangular palm shape and long, tapering fingers. Individuals with Water hands are emotionally sensitive, intuitive, and empathetic. They possess a deep understanding of human emotions and are highly perceptive of the feelings of others.

People with Water hands are often drawn to creative pursuits and have a natural talent for artistic expression, music, and healing arts. Their heightened intuition guides them in decision-making, and they are attuned to the subtle energies of the world around them. Water hands are associated with qualities such as adaptability, receptivity, and a nurturing nature.

The Fire Hand: Passion and Energy

The Fire hand is characterized by its palm shape, which is longer than it is wide, and its short, strong fingers. Those with Fire hands are passionate, energetic, and driven individuals. They have a zest for life and are always seeking new challenges and opportunities.

People with Fire hands are natural leaders and possess a strong desire to make a positive impact on the world. They excel in fields that require charisma, motivation, and a competitive spirit. Fire hands are associated with qualities such as creativity, assertiveness, and a magnetic presence that draws others to them.

The Air Hand: Intellect and Communication

The Air hand is identified by its square-shaped palm with long, slender fingers. Individuals with Air hands are known for their analytical minds, quick wit, and excellent communication skills. They have a love for knowledge and enjoy intellectual pursuits and learning.

People with Air hands are often drawn to fields such as writing, teaching, and research. They have a talent for problem-solving and excel in tasks that require logical thinking and clear communication. Air hands are associated with qualities such as adaptability, objectivity, and a strong sense of curiosity.

Hand Combinations: Embracing Complexity

While each hand shape has its unique characteristics, most individuals have hand combinations that include elements of multiple shapes. A person may have a dominant hand shape while also displaying characteristics of other shapes, creating a more intricate and multifaceted personality profile.

Hand combinations in palmistry are fascinating because they reveal the complexities and richness of human nature. For example, an individual may have an Earth hand with practicality and stability as the dominant traits, combined with Water hand characteristics of emotional sensitivity and creativity. Such combinations create unique and versatile personalities that embody a range of qualities and strengths.

The Influence of Hand Shapes on Life Paths

Understanding hand shapes and their impact on an individual's life path can provide valuable guidance in making life decisions. For instance:

Earth hands may thrive in stable and conventional careers, finding fulfillment in practical professions that allow them to contribute tangibly to society.

Water hands may excel in artistic and healing professions, drawn to creative fields that allow them to connect emotionally with others.

Fire hands may seek leadership roles and ambitious pursuits, driven by their passion to leave a mark on the world.

Air hands may gravitate towards intellectual and communicative fields, finding fulfillment in careers that involve critical thinking and expression.

It is essential to approach hand shape analysis with sensitivity and an understanding that every individual is unique, influenced by various factors beyond hand shapes. Palmistry, when combined with intuition and open-mindedness, offers a valuable tool for self-awareness, personal growth, and a deeper understanding of the complex and beautiful tapestry of human diversity. As we delve into the diverse hand shapes and their implications, let us celebrate the intricacies of the human hand and the extraordinary potential it holds.

CASE STUDY: GEORGE GERSHWIN

American Composer George Gershwin, was born on September 26, 1898, in Brooklyn, New York, and died on July 11, 1937, in Hollywood, California. He was a prominent American composer renowned for his Broadway musical theater compositions, he skillfully blended classical music techniques with popular music and jazz elements.

The son of Russian Jewish immigrants, Gershwin's musical journey began at age 11 when his family purchased a piano for his brother, Ira. However, George's natural talent quickly became apparent. He received lessons from Charles Hambitzer, who recognized his genius, and continued to expand his musical knowledge under various mentors, including Henry Cowell and Joseph Schillinger.

Leaving school at 15, Gershwin made piano rolls and played in nightclubs. His stint as a song plugger for the Jerome Remick music-publishing company was a significant early career step. Despite the demanding nature of this job, it honed his skills in improvisation and transposition.

Gershwin's first published song, "When You Want 'Em You Can't Get 'Em (When You've Got 'Em You Don't Want 'Em)," came out in 1916, along with his first piano composition, "Rialto Ripples." His work caught the attention of Broadway figures, leading to his songs being included in shows like The Passing Show of 1916.

Influenced by Irving Berlin and Jerome Kern, Gershwin aspired to compose for Broadway. His big break came in 1919 when Al Jolson performed his song "Swanee" in the musical Sinbad, catapulting Gershwin to fame. That year, he also composed the entire score for La, La Lucille and his first serious work, the Lullaby for string quartet.

From 1920 to 1924, Gershwin wrote scores for George White's Scandals, producing hits like "(I'll Build a) Stairway to Paradise." His one-act jazz opera, Blue Monday, was initially unsuccessful but caught the attention of bandleader Paul Whiteman. In 1924, at Whiteman's request, Gershwin composed Rhapsody in Blue, a piece blending jazz and classical elements, in just three weeks. This work became one of his most famous compositions, solidifying his status as a significant figure in American music.

Adapted from the character sketch from impressions of the hands of George Gershwin by Nellie Simmons Meier

Nellie made the statement that George Gershwin brought jazz to the attention of the musical intelligentsia or brought the musical intelligentsia down to noticing jazz, depending on whether one belonged to the group of analytical musicians who enjoyed scrutinizing compositions and techniques for flaws, or the majority who loved music for its melodic appeal and rhythmic quality.

She met Mr. Gershwin in June of 1933, intrigued to examine his hands due to the recognition he had received from the public for his musical compositions at a relatively early age.

Mr. Gershwin's handshake was unforgettable, reflecting the decisiveness and personality found in some of his dramatic musical climaxes. It conveyed directness and efficiency, suggesting that getting straight to the point would yield the best results.

His thumbs, not overly flexible at the first joint, indicated a surface adaptability when interacting with people who didn't particularly interest him. The shape of his thumbs showed a dominant will over logic and reason, a trait that drove him to overcome significant obstacles and persist despite logical reasons to abandon his plans. This will, combined with a slight flexibility in the joint, demonstrated an adaptability necessary for public demands.

The second joint of his thumb revealed the reason and logic he employed once his strong will had helped him overcome irritability caused by interruptions or delays in his work.

The firmness of his palm added strength to his will. Whether this characteristic furthered his career or created obstacles depended on him. If he let the pride indicated by the mount under his first finger and his super-sensitivity, as shown by the high cushions on the nail phalanges, govern his actions, he risked arousing opposition and creating unnecessary barriers. Conversely, these traits could help him overcome adverse conditions.

The pointed tips of his first fingers showed quick perception, aiding him in seizing opportunities to advance his ambitions and love of power. The length of the nail phalange of his first finger denoted sincerity, a convincing quality in his work, explaining his perseverance in following his unique compositional style.

The middle phalanges revealed a sense of uncompromising justice in critiquing his work, being his own harshest critic. The length of the nail phalanges of his second fingers showed earnestness in his work, with the square tip indicating a desire for reasoned results.

The prudence in the second phalange of his middle finger could become excessive caution, potentially hindering his efforts, if not balanced by the reason shown in the square tip.

The long first phalange of his third finger, indicating a love of lines, combined with the spatulate tip, highlighted his gift for composition and originality in challenging traditional musical expressions. He was a law unto himself, confident in his ideas.

The length of the middle phalange of his third finger, related to color, illustrated his ability to indicate moods lightly rather than letting them become dominant. His fourth finger's length showed diplomacy, essential in handling personal, professional, or commercial discord.

The length of the first phalange of his fourth finger, with a rounded tip, displayed his talent as an instrumentalist and composer. The development of the third phalange of his thumb, the mount of Venus, and the mount of Luna, emphasized strong melodic and rhythmic qualities, further accentuated by the markings on the mount of the Moon, intensifying his imaginative faculties in musical expression.

The flare between his first and second fingers, denoting independent thought, and between his third and fourth fingers, indicating independent action, were powerful forces in his colorful, tuneful, and imaginative compositions. While Gershwin was distinctly independent as a composer, the length of the middle phalanges of his fingers revealed a solid foundation of musical knowledge and technique.

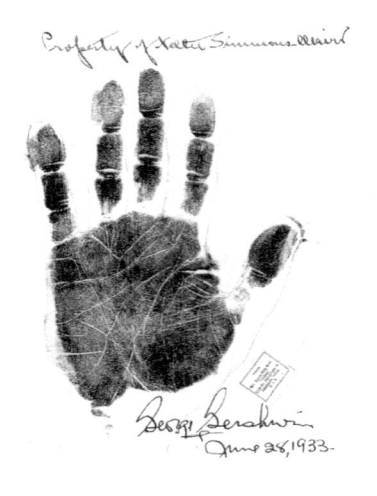

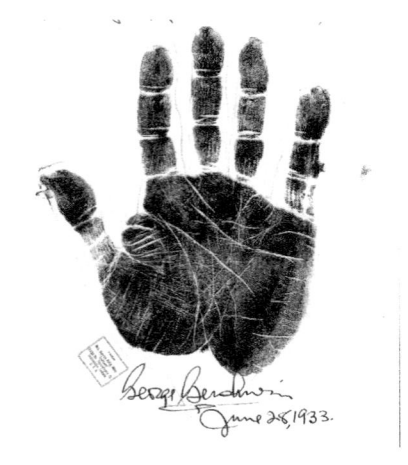

CHAPTER 5

The Major Lines

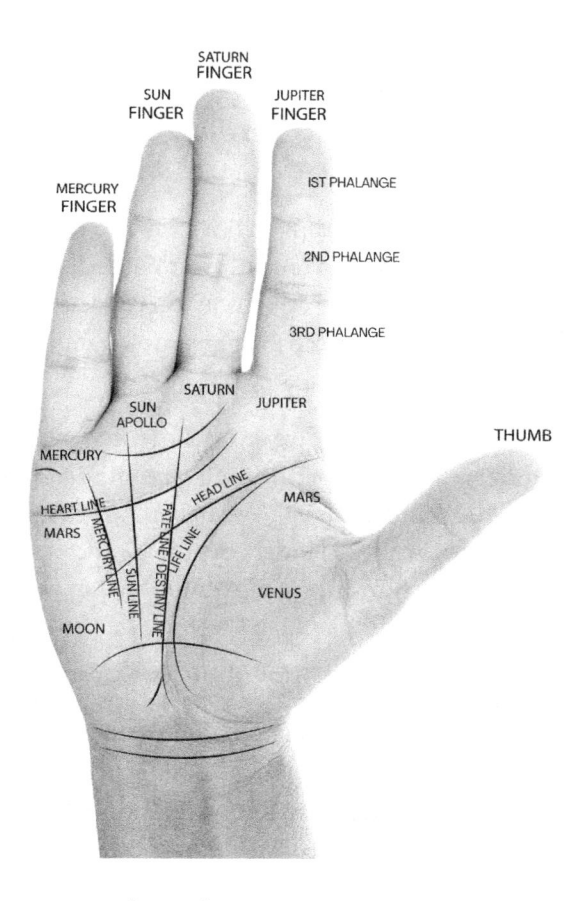

Reading the Major Lines

- **The Heart Line**: Meaning, variations, and interpretations
- **The Head Line**: Understanding thought processes and intellectual tendencies

- **The Life Line**: Insights into vitality, health, and life journey
- **The Fate Line**: Destiny, career, and life path

In palmistry, the major lines on the hand provide profound insights into an individual's personality, experiences, and life path. As we embark on the journey of reading the major lines, we uncover the hidden stories etched into the palm, revealing the mysteries of the past, present, and future.

The Life Line: Mapping Vitality and Life's Journey

The Life Line, one of the primary lines on the hand, arcs around the base of the thumb and extends towards the wrist. Contrary to popular belief, the Life Line does not foretell the length of one's life. Instead, it provides valuable insights into an individual's vitality, energy levels, and overall well-being.

As we explore the Life Line, we learn how its length, depth, and interruptions can indicate periods of strength and resilience or times of challenges and changes. We delve into the significance of variations, such as breaks, islands, and forks, and how they reflect significant life events, transitions, and emotional experiences.

The Head Line: Deciphering Thought Processes and Intellect

The Head Line, running horizontally across the palm, represents the mind and thought processes. This line provides clues about an individual's intellectual capacity, decision-making style, and approach to problem-solving.

In this section, we delve into the varying lengths, shapes, and slopes of the Head Line, deciphering their meanings. We explore how a straight and clear Head Line reflects logical thinking and a practical approach, while a wavy or curved line suggests a more imaginative and intuitive nature. We also discuss the significance of forks, islands, and other markings, which can indicate periods of mental focus or distractions.

The Heart Line: Unraveling Emotions and Relationships

The Heart Line, curving above the Head Line, reveals an individual's emotional experiences, romantic inclinations, and approach to relationships. It serves as a window into the depths of one's emotional world.

In this segment, we explore how the length and depth of the Heart Line relate to an individual's emotional sensitivity, capacity for love, and ability to express affection. We also examine the significance of breaks, forks, and islands, which may indicate periods of emotional turbulence or transformative romantic experiences.

The Fate Line: Tracing Life's Path and Achievements

The Fate Line, also known as the Line of Destiny, vertically crosses the center of the palm. It provides insights into an individual's life path, career trajectory, and the influence of external circumstances on their journey.

As we explore the Fate Line, we decode its length, depth, and intersection with other lines to determine the individual's sense of purpose and the impact of life events on their career and personal achievements. We discuss how breaks, changes in direction, and other markings can signify significant shifts in one's life course and the potential for success and fulfillment.

The Sun Line: Unveiling Success and Accomplishments

The Sun Line, also known as the Apollo Line, vertically rises from the base of the palm towards the ring finger. This line is associated with achievements, recognition, and success in one's endeavors.

In this section, we explore the various forms and significance of the Sun Line, revealing an individual's potential for fame, creativity, and public recognition. We discuss how this line interacts with other major lines, providing insights into the individual's ambitions and their journey towards success and self-actualization.

Interpreting Multiple Lines: A Holistic Approach

Beyond analyzing each major line individually, we emphasize the importance of interpreting these lines collectively. By examining how the major lines intersect, overlap, or diverge, we paint a more comprehensive picture of an individual's life experiences, personality, and potential.

Throughout this section, we provide real-life examples and case studies to demonstrate the art of reading the major lines and the intricate interplay between these lines. We encourage readers to approach palmistry with an open mind and an understanding that the lines on the hand are not fixed or deterministic but instead offer valuable guidance for self-awareness and personal growth.

In embracing the journey of reading the major lines, we embark on a voyage of self-discovery and wisdom, unraveling the mysteries concealed within the lines of the human hand. As we peel back the layers of each line, we celebrate the profound insights palmistry offers into the depths of the human soul and the intricate tapestry of our life's journey.

CASE STUDY: MARGARET SANGER

Pioneer of Reproductive Rights

Margaret Sanger (1879-1966) was a leading advocate for women's reproductive rights and the founder of Planned Parenthood. Raised in a working-class family, her experiences with poverty and unwanted pregnancies drove her to champion birth control. In 1916, she opened the first U.S. birth control clinic, facing legal challenges. She founded the American Birth Control League in 1921, later evolving into Planned Parenthood. Sanger's tireless efforts contributed to the legalization of contraception in the U.S. Her legacy, though controversial due to early eugenic associations, is celebrated for expanding access to reproductive healthcare.

Adapted from the hand readings of Margaret Sanger by Mrs. George Philip Meier December 15, 1933

In the two decades preceding her palm reading, Margaret Sanger faced unparalleled challenges and criticism in the United States. Despite this, she remained unwavering in her mission to ensure that future generations were born to informed and prepared parents. When she visited for her palm reading, NSM was already familiar with her dedication and personal journey. Sanger's early life was marked by witnessing her mother's hardships due to frequent pregnancies. This experience, reflected in her palms, was a catalyst for her groundbreaking work.

Upon examining Sanger's hands, the circles of intuition were unmistakable in both. These arcs, starting under the Mount of Mercury and stretching to the Mount of the Moon, revealed her innate intuitive abilities. The unique patterns of capillaries on her palms, which Nellie Simmons Meier referred to as "thumb prints" on Luna, were indicative of her deep intuitive gifts. These patterns were not just on the Mount of the Moon but also between her fingers, signaling her exceptional intuition.

Margaret Sanger's approach to her work was largely instinctive. She absorbed impressions and formulated plans subconsciously, often finding herself with a clear, inevitable course of action laid out before her. Her handshake, firm and sincere, was a testament to her ability to immediately connect with and understand others. The resilience of her palm was extraordinary, allowing her to intuitively sense a person's mood and opinions through mere touch.

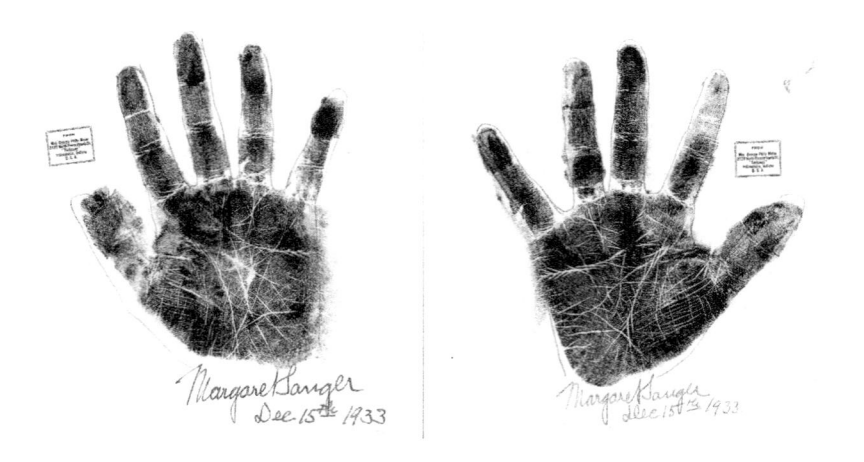

The pronounced Mount of Venus in her hand, along with the downward slope of her headline towards the Mount of the Moon in her left hand, highlighted her empathy and imagination. However, this sometimes clouded her judgment, leading to periods of depression due to perceived stagnation in her efforts. The straight headline in her right hand indicated growing confidence over time. The development of the Mount of Jupiter suggested a modest desire for recognition, but it was not her primary driving force.

Sanger's motivation and driving power stemmed from her impulsive nature, deep empathy, and her extraordinary intuitive sense. She was a reformer not driven by self-interest but by a genuine desire to effect change. Her success, despite the immense challenges she faced, can be attributed to her unique intuitive qualities, which enabled her to seize the right moment to advance her cause.

CHAPTER 6

The Minor Lines

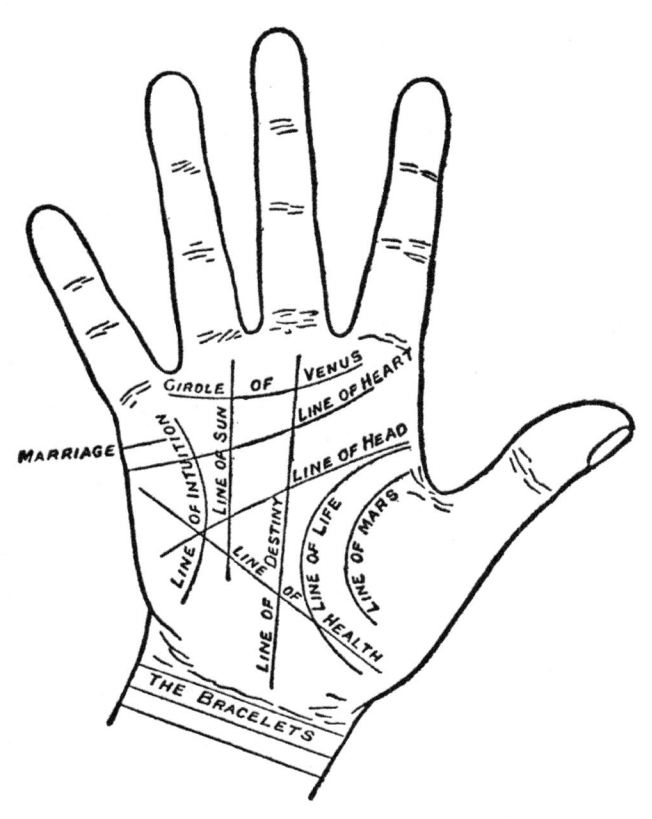

This illustration is from the book "Palmistry for All" by Cheiro (1866-1936), published in May, 1916.

The Sun Line: Fame, success, and creativity
The Mercury Line: Communication skills and business acumen
The Marriage Lines: Relationships and unions
Other minor lines and their significance

Unveiling the Minor Lines and Marks in Palmistry

Welcome to the intriguing world of minor lines and marks in palmistry! In this chapter, we delve deeper into the intricate details etched on the human hand, exploring the significance of minor lines and marks that enrich the art of palmistry. These lines and marks provide additional insights into an individual's personality traits, experiences, and potential life paths. As we unveil the mysteries hidden within the palm, we gain a more comprehensive understanding of the complexities of human nature.

The Mercury Line: Communication and Intuition

The Mercury Line, also known as the Health Line or Line of Intuition, runs horizontally across the palm below the little finger. This line is associated with communication skills, intuition, and mental agility.

In this section, we explore the various forms and lengths of the Mercury Line, decoding their meanings. We examine how a strong and unbroken Mercury Line indicates excellent communication abilities and a sharp intuition. Additionally, we delve into the significance of any breaks or markings on the Mercury Line, which may reveal periods of health issues or moments of intuitive awakening.

The Saturn Line: Order and Responsibility

The Saturn Line, also called the Line of Duty or Fate Line Variant, is a vertical line that rises from the wrist towards the middle finger. This line represents a person's sense of responsibility, discipline, and work ethic.

As we unveil the Saturn Line, we interpret its length, depth, and intersections with other lines to understand an individual's approach to responsibilities and career choices. We discuss how a well-developed Saturn Line signifies a strong sense of duty and a structured approach to life. Additionally, we explore the implications of any interruptions or markings on this line, which may indicate significant life changes or periods of self-discovery.

The Apollo Line: Creativity and Expression

The Apollo Line, also known as the Line of Sun or the Sister Line to the Fate Line, runs parallel to the Fate Line or Sun Line. This line is associated with creativity, artistic talents, and the pursuit of passions.

In this section, we uncover the meaning behind the Apollo Line and its connection to the individual's desire for self-expression and creative endeavors. We explore how a prominent and well-defined Apollo Line indicates a passion for the arts and a flair for creative pursuits. We also discuss the potential impact of any markings or intersections on the Apollo Line, revealing periods of artistic growth or recognition.

The Girdle of Venus: Sensitivity and Emotions

The Girdle of Venus is a semi-circular line that starts between the index and middle fingers and arches across the palm, reaching the little finger. This line is linked to an individual's emotional intensity, sensitivity, and intuitive nature.

As we unveil the Girdle of Venus, we explore how its presence may suggest heightened emotional sensitivity and deep emotional experiences. We discuss the potential significance of a well-defined and uninterrupted Girdle of Venus, as well as any breaks or markings on this line that may indicate emotional challenges or transformative emotional growth.

Special Marks and Symbols: Messages from the Hand

Beyond the minor lines, the hand may bear various marks, symbols, and mounts that provide additional layers of meaning to the palmistry analysis. These marks can include stars, crosses, triangles, and other unique symbols, each carrying its own significance.

In this section, we embark on a journey to decipher the language of these special marks and symbols, uncovering their hidden messages and implications for the individual's life path and experiences. We emphasize the importance of considering these symbols in the context of the entire hand, recognizing that their meanings can vary based on their location and relationship with other lines and features.

The Art of Reading Minor Lines and Marks

Reading the minor lines and marks requires attention to detail, intuition, and a holistic understanding of the hand. Throughout this chapter, we provide practical tips and insights to help readers develop their skills in interpreting minor lines and marks effectively. We encourage practitioners to approach palmistry with reverence and respect for the unique stories inscribed on each hand, embracing the art's transformative potential for self-awareness and personal growth.

As we unveil the minor lines and marks in palmistry, we celebrate the richness and complexity of human nature, each hand a unique canvas of experiences and potentials. With an open heart and a curious mind, we continue our exploration of the profound wisdom held within the lines of the human hand, gaining deeper insights into the intricacies of the human soul.

CASE STUDY: AMELIA EARHART

American Aviator Amelia Earhart, was born on July 24, 1897, in Atchison, Kansas, and disappeared on July 2, 1937, near Howland Island in the Pacific. She was a celebrated American aviator and the first woman to fly solo across the Atlantic Ocean. Her 1937 disappearance during a global flight attempt remains a mystery and a subject of speculation.

Earhart, whose father was a railroad lawyer and mother from a wealthy family, showed independence and adventure from a young age. After financial struggles and her father's alcoholism, she finished high school in Chicago in 1916. Post her mother's inheritance, Earhart attended the Ogontz School in Pennsylvania but left to become a nurse's aide in Toronto during World War I.

In the 1920s, after a brief stint in premed at Columbia University and a move to California, Earhart's first flight experience in 1920 led her to pursue aviation. She bought her first plane in 1921 and earned her pilot's license in 1923. Later, she moved to Massachusetts, working as a social worker while continuing flying.

Earhart gained fame after being chosen for a transatlantic flight in 1928, partly due to her resemblance to Charles Lindbergh. She flew from Newfoundland to Wales with pilots Wilmer Stultz and Louis Gordon, becoming an international celebrity. She married publisher George Palmer Putnam in 1931, who had organized the flight, but retained her maiden name professionally.

In 1932, Earhart solo flew across the Atlantic from Newfoundland to Northern Ireland in under 15 hours, despite challenges. She continued to break records, including the first solo flight from Hawaii to California in 1935 and from Los Angeles to Mexico City.

Earhart embarked on a world flight in 1937 with navigator Fred Noonan, covering 22,000 miles before disappearing en route to Howland Island. Despite a massive search, she and Noonan were declared lost at sea. Earhart's letters and diary entries from the trip were published posthumously in "Last Flight" (1937).

Her disappearance led to various theories, including crash-landing on a different island or capture by the Japanese, but no conclusive evidence supports these. Most experts believe her plane crashed near Howland Island due to fuel shortage. Earhart remains a significant figure in popular culture, inspiring numerous books and films.

Adapted from the Character Sketch from impressions of the hands of Amelia Earhart by Nellie Simmons-Meier, June 28, 1933

In exploring the hands of notable aviators, Amelia Earhart, the first woman to fly solo across the Atlantic, stood out. Nellie was keen to understand the hand characteristics that contributed to her remarkable achievements and her sustained public interest as an aviator.

Earhart's long palm suggested a love for physical activity, while her long fingers indicated meticulousness in planning and executing her goals. The joining of her lifeline and headline showed her cautious approach, especially in personal enterprises, preventing unnecessary risks. Her thumb's first phalange highlighted a strong, potentially stubborn will, tempered by the logic indicated in the second phalange.

The second phalange's shape pointed to mental agility, crucial for quick decision-making. Her smooth fingers and straight headline denoted the inspiration needed for emergency responses during flights. Her long first fingers revealed executive ability, ambition, and a preference for genuine praise over flattery.

Her long, straight headline ensured that her ambition was balanced by clear vision, not clouded by flattery. The unusual length of her fourth finger suggested diplomacy, kept in check by a strong sense of conscience. The spacing between her thumbs and fingers, along with her nail shape, indicated impatience with restrictions, often leading her to seek freedom through flying.

Earhart's hand showed a blend of courage and caution. Her right hand's headline displayed mental strength and focus, supported by a stiff thumb and a strong will. Her courage, dictated by mental faculties, was evident in the Upper Mount of Mars development, classifying her hand as a mental type.

Her hand's length and breadth reaffirmed her physical activity passion, while her long fingers underscored her attention to detail. Signs of caution were repeated throughout her hand – the close life and headline connection, the reasoned and logical second phalanges, and the conscientious fourth finger. These traits underscored her tendency to carefully consider decisions.

Her right thumb's second phalange again emphasized mental agility, allowing for swift decisions when necessary. A notable quality was her ability to discern genuine admiration from flattery, thanks to her clear, analytical thinking. Her ambition was balanced by a desire for clarity and truth, preventing her from being swayed by insincere praise. Her hands reflected a person who sought clarity and was driven by a blend of ambition, caution, and mental acuity.

Amelia Earhart, June 28, 1933.

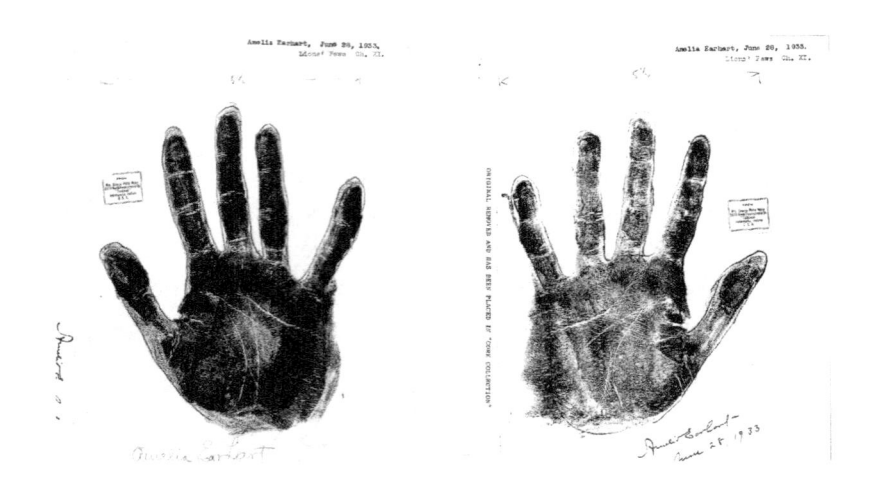

CHAPTER 7

The Mounts

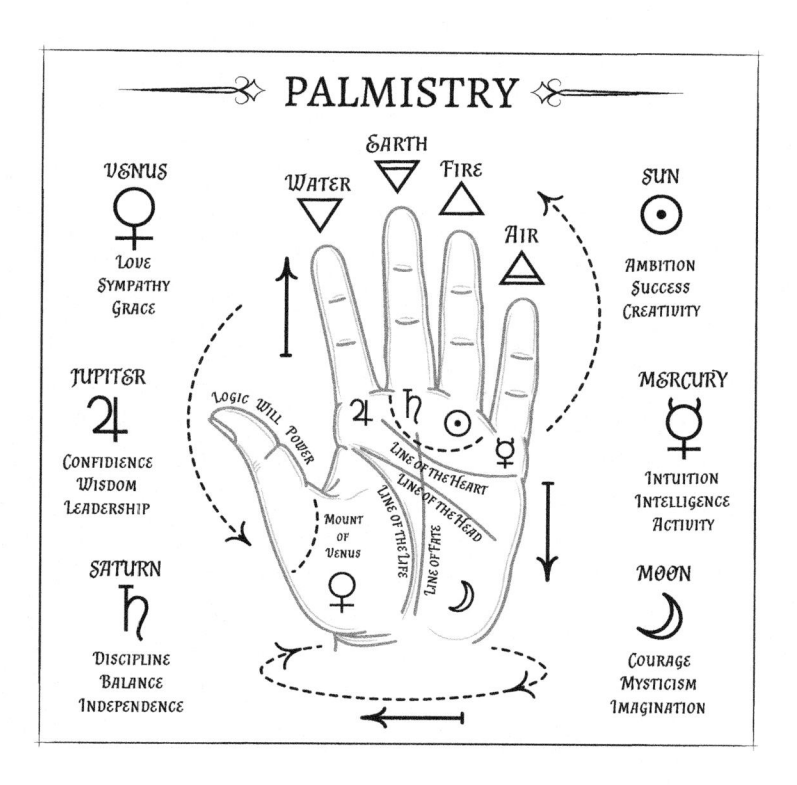

The Celestial Connection of Palmistry

For millennia, the art of palmistry, often referred to as chiromancy, has captivated the minds of seekers, offering a window into the depths of one's character, potential, and the path ahead. While the intricate lines that weave across the palm often draw the most attention, they are but one aspect of this profound discipline.

Equally significant are the mounts—those raised sections of the palm that hold their own tales and secrets. Intriguingly, these mounts bear the names of celestial entities, underscoring the ancient and enduring belief in the intricate dance between the vast cosmos and the individual soul. As we journey through this chapter, we will embark on an exploration of the profound meanings and insights offered by the seven pivotal mounts: Jupiter, Saturn, Apollo, Mercury, Mars, Moon, and Venus.

Mount of Jupiter: The Emblem of Leadership and Ambition

Situated prominently at the base of the index finger, just above the Mount of Mars, the Mount of Jupiter holds a special place in the realm of palmistry. This mount, named after the king of the Roman gods, is deeply intertwined with qualities of leadership, ambition, and honor. Its position on the hand, close to the index finger, is symbolic of its association with authority and direction.

A well-defined Mount of Jupiter is a testament to an individual's innate leadership qualities. Such a person doesn't just crave power for the sake of it; they are driven by a deeper purpose. Their ambition is fueled by a genuine desire to make a positive impact on society, to lead by example, and to inspire others. These individuals often find themselves in positions of authority, not because they seek it, but because others naturally gravitate towards their guiding light. They have an inherent ability to rally people around a cause, making them effective leaders in various spheres, be it in business, politics, or community service.

Moreover, the Mount of Jupiter is also a symbol of honor. Those with a pronounced mount are often individuals of integrity. They value their reputation and are guided by a moral compass that ensures they act justly and fairly. Their word is their bond, and they often go to great lengths to uphold promises and commitments.

However, like all things, there's a balance to be maintained. If the Mount of Jupiter is overly pronounced or has certain markings, it can indicate potential pitfalls. Such an exaggerated mount might hint at a person's tendency to be arrogant or domineering. They might have an inflated sense of self-worth, believing that their way is the only right way. This can lead to conflicts, as they may come across as overbearing or dismissive of others' opinions.

The Mount of Jupiter is a powerful indicator of leadership qualities, ambition, and honor in an individual. While it signifies many positive traits, it's essential to be aware of its potential negative manifestations. As with all aspects of palmistry, understanding the nuances of the Mount of Jupiter can offer valuable insights into one's character and life journey.

Mount of Saturn: The Realm of Deep Reflection and Wisdom

Nestled at the base of the middle finger lies the Mount of Saturn, a significant landmark in the topography of the palm. This mount, named after the Roman god of time and agriculture, carries with it the weight of introspection, wisdom, and a natural inclination towards solitude.

Individuals with a pronounced Mount of Saturn are not just casual thinkers; they dive deep into the abyss of thought, often getting lost in the vast landscapes of their minds. Their attraction to life's mysteries isn't merely a fleeting curiosity; it's a profound quest for understanding. This quest often leads them down paths less traveled, where they seek answers to existential questions and the greater truths of the universe.

Their philosophical inclinations are evident in their conversations and reflections. They are the ones who, amidst casual chatter, will pose thought-provoking questions, urging those around them to think beyond the superficial. This depth of thought is complemented by their patience. They understand that true wisdom doesn't come in an instant but is cultivated over time, through experiences, reflections, and continuous learning.

Moreover, their persistence is noteworthy. Whether it's a challenging puzzle, a complex theory, or a personal endeavor, they approach it with unwavering determination, often working silently in the background until they achieve their goal.

Yet, every strength can also be a potential weakness if taken to an extreme. An excessively prominent Mount of Saturn can hint at potential challenges. Such individuals might grapple with feelings of melancholy, often feeling weighed down by their own thoughts. Their natural inclination towards introspection can sometimes spiral into excessive introversion, making them distant or detached from the world around them. They might struggle to connect with others, preferring the company of their thoughts over social interactions.

The Mount of Saturn is a testament to the profound thinkers among us, those who seek wisdom and understanding beyond the surface. While it brings with it many admirable qualities, it's essential to strike a balance, ensuring that introspection doesn't lead to isolation.

Mount of Apollo: The Luminous Beacon of Artistry and Charm

Positioned gracefully at the base of the ring finger, the Mount of Apollo, often synonymous with the Sun Mount, shines brightly in the realm of palmistry. Drawing its name from Apollo, the ancient Greek god of music, arts, and the sun, this mount embodies the radiant qualities of creativity, charisma, and unparalleled artistic prowess.

Individuals blessed with a prominent Mount of Apollo are not merely creative; they are the embodiment of artistic expression. Their souls resonate with the rhythms of music, the strokes of a paintbrush, the elegance of dance, and the poetic cadence of words. This intrinsic connection to the arts is often evident from a young age, as they are naturally drawn to colors, sounds, and movements, finding joy and purpose in artistic expression.

Beyond their artistic talents, these individuals radiate an optimism that is both infectious and uplifting. They view the world through a lens of possibilities, seeing beauty in the mundane and finding inspiration in the everyday. This sunny disposition often makes them magnets for positive energy, drawing people towards them effortlessly.

Their charisma is undeniable. Whether they're stepping onto a stage, entering a room, or merely striking up a conversation, they possess a magnetic charm that captivates audiences and endears them to others. It's not just about being the center of attention; it's about lighting up the space around them, making others feel seen, heard, and valued.

However, not every Mount of Apollo is pronounced, and an underdeveloped one carries its own set of implications. Such a mount might hint at an individual's uncertainty or lack of confidence in their creative potential. They might harbor latent talents but are held back by self-doubt or fear of judgment. It's essential for them to recognize that creativity is a journey, and with encouragement and practice, they can hone their skills and let their inner artist shine.

In essence, the Mount of Apollo is a testament to the vibrant tapestry of creativity and charisma that some individuals are endowed with. It reminds us of the power of art to inspire, the allure of genuine charisma, and the importance of believing in one's creative gifts.

Mount of Mercury: The Nexus of Eloquence and Insight

Perched at the base of the little finger, the Mount of Mercury stands as a sentinel of swift thought and eloquent expression. Named after Mercury, the Roman god of communication, commerce, and cunning, this mount encapsulates the intricate dance of words, intuition, and strategic acumen.

Individuals graced with a prominent Mount of Mercury are not just communicators; they are masterful orators and writers, weaving words with precision and intent. Their ability to articulate thoughts, emotions, and ideas is unparalleled, making them stand out in debates, discussions, and dialogues. Whether it's penning a compelling narrative or delivering a captivating speech, their gift of gab is evident.

Beyond mere communication, their intuitive faculties are heightened. They possess an uncanny ability to 'read the room,' sensing underlying currents and emotions, often before they are verbally expressed. This intuitive edge, combined with their communicative prowess, makes them formidable negotiators and diplomats, able to navigate complex situations with ease.

Their sharp intellect is also reflected in their business acumen. The world of commerce and trade is not just about numbers and transactions for them; it's a chessboard where strategy, foresight, and communication converge. They can anticipate market trends, understand consumer behavior, and craft persuasive pitches, making them invaluable assets in the business arena.

However, every strength, when taken to an extreme, can manifest as a potential weakness. An overly developed Mount of Mercury can be a double-edged sword. While it amplifies the qualities mentioned, it can also hint at a propensity for cunning or deceit. Such individuals might use their gift of communication for manipulation, spinning webs of half-truths or misdirection. It's crucial to approach such indications with caution, understanding that while the mount provides insights, it doesn't define one's character in its entirety.

The Mount of Mercury is a fascinating blend of eloquence, intuition, and strategic insight. It underscores the power of effective communication and the importance of using one's gifts responsibly and ethically.

Mount of Mars: The Dual Facets of Courage and Temperament

Situated within the intricate landscape of the palm, the Mount of Mars stands out due to its bifurcated nature. Unlike other mounts, Mars is split into two distinct regions, each holding its own set of characteristics and insights. This duality mirrors the complexities of human nature, where courage coexists with aggression, and resilience intertwines with volatility.

The Upper Mars, nestled between the mounts of Jupiter and Saturn, is a beacon of bravery and tenacity. It symbolizes the indomitable spirit that rises in the face of adversity. Individuals with a pronounced Upper Mars are not easily deterred by challenges. They possess a warrior-like spirit, ready to face obstacles head-on with unwavering determination. This resilience often manifests in various aspects of their lives, be it personal challenges, professional hurdles, or emotional battles. They are the ones who, when knocked down, rise with even more vigor and resolve.

Conversely, the Lower Mars, positioned between the mounts of Venus and Moon, delves into the more tempestuous aspects of one's character. It is the realm of raw emotion, particularly temper and aggression. A pronounced Lower Mars suggests an individual with a fiery disposition, quick to react and often driven by impulse. While this can translate to passion and zeal in certain situations, unchecked, it can lead to confrontations and conflicts.

A harmonious balance between the Upper and Lower Mars is the ideal. Such a balance indicates an individual who embodies the best of both worlds. They are brave and resilient, ready to face life's challenges with courage, yet they also possess the wisdom to control their temper, channeling their energy constructively. They know when to stand firm and when to step back, making them both formidable and approachable.

However, an imbalance, where one mount overshadows the other, can lead to challenges. An overly dominant Upper Mars might make one overly defiant, sometimes to the point of recklessness. In contrast, an exaggerated Lower Mars might indicate a person prone to outbursts, impulsiveness, and potential aggression.

In essence, the Mount of Mars, with its dual facets, offers a profound insight into the dance of courage and temperament within an individual. It serves as a reminder of the delicate balance one must maintain to navigate life with both strength and grace.

Mount of Moon: The Odyssey of Imagination and Intuition

Resting on the farthest edge of the palm, opposite the thumb, the Mount of Moon, often referred to as the Lunar Mount, stands as a testament to the dreamers, the intuitives, and the explorers of the world. This mount, bathed in the ethereal glow of its celestial namesake, encapsulates the vast realms of imagination, the subtle nudges of intuition, and the insatiable desire to journey beyond the familiar.

A well-defined Mount of Moon is like a boundless ocean of creativity and insight. Individuals with such a mount are often daydreamers, their minds a canvas of vivid imaginations, where fantasies come to life and ideas take flight. They are the storytellers, the artists, and the visionaries, seeing possibilities where others see limits.

Beyond imagination, their intuitive faculties are finely tuned, allowing them to perceive nuances and subtleties that might elude others. This intuitive prowess often manifests in various ways – from understanding unspoken emotions to anticipating events before they unfold. They are the ones who often rely on their 'gut feelings,' guided by an inner compass that rarely steers them wrong.

The Mount of Moon also resonates with the spirit of adventure and exploration. Those with a pronounced mount are not just content with the known; they are drawn to the mysteries of the uncharted.

This wanderlust can be literal, manifesting as a desire to travel and explore diverse cultures and landscapes. Alternatively, it can be metaphorical, representing a quest for knowledge, understanding, and personal growth.

However, not all Mounts of Moon are pronounced, and an underdeveloped one carries its own tales. Such a mount might hint at challenges in the emotional realm. Individuals might struggle with empathy, finding it hard to resonate with others' feelings or emotions. This can lead to misunderstandings or perceived aloofness, as they might inadvertently come across as distant or detached.

The Mount of Moon is a fascinating blend of the ethereal and the tangible, bridging the gap between dreams and reality. It serves as a reminder of the power of imagination, the trustworthiness of intuition, and the beauty of exploration. Whether one is journeying through the landscapes of the mind or the terrains of the world, the Mount of Moon lights the way.

Mount of Venus: The Wellspring of Passion and Compassion

Anchored firmly at the base of the thumb, the Mount of Venus stands as a symbol of the heart's deepest desires and emotions. Named after Venus, the Roman goddess of love, beauty, and fertility, this mount embodies the fervor of passion, the warmth of compassion, and the allure of sensuality.

A pronounced Mount of Venus is a testament to an individual's rich emotional landscape. Such individuals are not just observers of life; they immerse themselves in its tapestry, feeling every thread of joy, love, and beauty. Their hearts are attuned to the rhythms of compassion, making them empathetic listeners and caring companions. They have an innate ability to resonate with others' emotions, offering comfort and understanding in times of need.

Their appreciation for life's pleasures is evident in their daily pursuits. They are the ones who stop to smell the roses, savor the flavors of a gourmet meal, or lose themselves in the melodies of a soulful tune. This zest for life is complemented by their keen sense of beauty, both in the physical and abstract realms. Whether it's the aesthetics of art, the harmony of nature, or the beauty in human connections, they recognize and cherish it.

Tactility is another hallmark of those with a well-defined Mount of Venus. They are often drawn to experiences that engage the senses. The softness of a fabric, the warmth of a hug, or the gentle caress of a breeze – such sensations are not just felt; they are celebrated. This tactile nature often translates to their relationships, where physical comfort and intimacy hold significant value.

However, as with all aspects of palmistry, extremes can offer cautionary tales. An overly developed Mount of Venus might hint at potential pitfalls in one's character. Such individuals might struggle with overindulgence, seeking pleasure to the point of excess. This could manifest in various ways, from materialistic pursuits to hedonistic tendencies. Additionally, the intense emotions associated with this mount, when unchecked, might lead to feelings of jealousy or possessiveness, potentially straining relationships.

In essence, the Mount of Venus is a reflection of the heart's capacity to love, feel, and experience. It reminds us of the joys of passion and the responsibilities of compassion. While it celebrates the pleasures of life, it also cautions against the dangers of excess. Balancing these dualities ensures a life lived with both fervor and wisdom.

The mounts adorning our palms serve as intriguing windows into the essence of our being, revealing facets of our character and latent potential. Drawing connections between these mounts and their celestial counterparts deepens our understanding, shedding light on our innate strengths, hurdles, and life's path. While palmistry offers valuable insights, it's crucial to remember that it presents possibilities, not certainties. Ultimately, while our hands may hint at our destiny, the decisions we make play a pivotal role in sculpting our future.

CASE STUDY: ALEXANDER, GRAND DUKE OF RUSSIA

Grand Duke Alexander Mikhailovich of Russia (1866-1933), often known as "Sandro," was a prominent member of the Russian imperial family and a naval officer. Born on April 13, 1866, in Tbilisi, Georgia, he was the son of Grand Duke Michael Nikolaevich of Russia and a grandson of Tsar Nicholas I. His mother was Grand Duchess Olga Feodorovna, born Princess Cecily of Baden. Alexander grew up in the Caucasus and St. Petersburg, receiving a comprehensive education that included extensive naval training, reflecting the Romanov family's traditional association with the Russian Navy.

Alexander married Grand Duchess Xenia Alexandrovna of Russia, the sister of Tsar Nicholas II, in 1894, further strengthening his ties to the imperial family. The couple had seven children, and their marriage was considered harmonious and happy. As a member of the Romanov family, Alexander was close to the Russian court and had significant influence in the early years of Nicholas II's reign.

His naval career was distinguished, and he held several high-ranking positions in the Russian Navy. However, his career was not without controversy, particularly regarding his involvement in the development of the Russian naval fleet, where his efforts were met with mixed success.

Alexander was known for his liberal political views, which often put him at odds with the more conservative elements at court. He supported reforms and was an advocate for constitutional monarchy, which he believed was essential for Russia's progress. His views, however, were not always well-received, especially as the political climate in Russia became increasingly tense in the early 20th century.

During World War I, Alexander served in various capacities, including as an advisor to the Tsar. However, the Russian Revolution of 1917 dramatically changed his life. With the fall of the Romanov dynasty, Alexander, along with his family, faced a period of uncertainty and danger. They were initially placed under house arrest and later managed to escape Russia.

In exile, Alexander spent the remainder of his life in France, where he wrote his memoirs, "Once a Grand Duke" and "Always a Grand Duke," which provided valuable insights into the Romanov family and the final years of Imperial Russia. These works are often cited for their detailed account of the Russian imperial family, the navy, and the political upheavals of the time.

Grand Duke Alexander Mikhailovich passed away on February 26, 1933, in Roquebrune-Cap-Martin, France. His life spanned the final decades of the Russian Empire, and he remains a significant figure in the study of this period due to his unique position within the Romanov family and his involvement in key historical events.

Adapted from the character sketch from impressions of the hands of Alexander, Grand Duke of Russia, by Nellie Simmons Meier

In presenting the hands of Alexander, Grand Duke of Russia, we see a figure born not just into wealth and power but also into a life of formidable challenges. On April 14th, 1931, NSM made impressions of his hands in the studio of Serge Yourievitch, a renowned sculptor and Vice President of the Society of Psychology of France. The Grand Duke, standing tall at six foot three with an erect military posture, possessed large hands that reflected his strong mentality and vitality, even at the age of 65. Known for his savoir-faire and social ease, he was a valued addition to any social gathering.

His courtesy extended to providing NSM with tickets to a concert at Otto Kahn's home, benefiting Russian refugees. The event, featuring famous Russian artists, was both a financial and artistic success. The Grand Duke's square palms indicated his fit for a position of authority, showing traits of belief in custom, punctuality, orderliness, and a methodical approach to studies and knowledge retention. His strong will, evident in the first phalange of his thumb, was used to drive others' activities, justified by the outcomes achieved. His clear judgment and broad tolerance towards others' opinions and actions were marked by the headline in his left hand.

In his right hand, the drooping headline towards the Mount of Imagination and the long first phalange of his second finger suggested that life's sudden shifts from fortune to hardship had biased his judgment, bending logic and reason to his perspective.

His preference for outdoor life and sports was balanced with his duty calls. His long middle phalanges indicated a keen interest in the mental world and scientific research. A lover of music, his appreciation for rhythm and melody was evident, though his inherited responsibilities often hindered the development of these interests. His talents, as indicated by the star of Brilliancy in his left hand, were often overshadowed by the obligations of his position.

The Grand Duke's heritage forced him to channel his talents into appreciating others' gifts. His fingers' long first phalanges suggested quick perception and a desire for reason, a strong religious inclination tempered by a dominant mentality, and originality in technical invention and scientific discovery. His love for color was a national trait, reflected in his creative artistry.

Despite not being a natural diplomat, his expressive abilities in speech and writing were notable. Born to privilege, he had the potential for indulgence but was instead guided by a desire for spiritual enlightenment and an intelligently developed mentality.

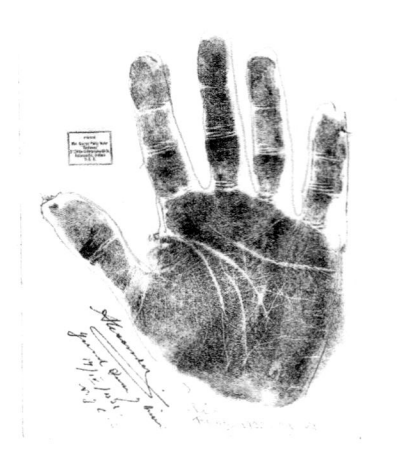

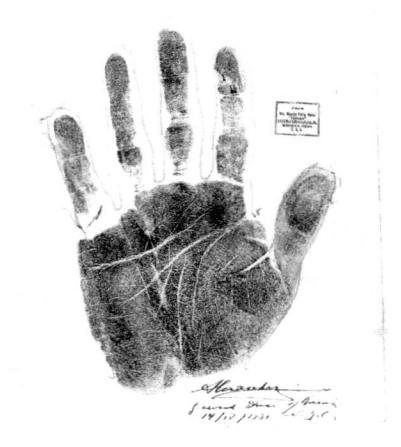

CHAPTER 8

Finger Analysis

The Meaning Behind Each Finger's Length and Shape in Palmistry

Palmistry, an ancient art rich in history and intrigue, delves deep into the lines and mounts of the hand to reveal insights about an individual's character and destiny. However, another equally significant aspect of palmistry is the study of the fingers – their length, their shape, and the stories they weave about one's personality and potential. Each finger, with its distinct characteristics, offers insights into different facets of an individual's nature.

The Thumb

The thumb, distinct from the fingers, holds a special place in palmistry. Representing one's willpower, logic, and ability to grasp various situations, its characteristics are telling.

Length: A long thumb suggests strong determination and a natural ability to lead. In contrast, a short thumb might indicate a more laid-back nature, with a preference for following rather than leading.

Shape: A flexible thumb speaks of adaptability and a willingness to embrace change, whereas a rigid thumb might hint at a more stubborn disposition.

Index Finger (Jupiter Finger)

This finger, associated with Jupiter, the Roman king of gods, speaks of ambition, leadership, and the quest for power.

Length: Individuals with a long index finger often have a strong drive for recognition and leadership. Those with a shorter index finger might be more content in supportive roles, shying away from the spotlight.

Shape: A straight index finger showcases confidence, while a bent one might indicate introspection and self-doubt.

Middle Finger (Saturn Finger)

Tied to the planet Saturn, the middle finger delves into themes of responsibility, balance, and one's attitude towards work.

Length: A pronounced middle finger suggests a serious and responsible nature, while a shorter one might hint at a more relaxed approach to life.

Shape: A straight middle finger indicates a balanced individual, but if it leans or bends, it might suggest a person who gravitates towards extremes.

Ring Finger (Apollo Finger)

Reflecting the god of arts, Apollo, the ring finger is a mirror to one's creative spirit and appreciation of beauty.

Length: A long ring finger is often found in those with a strong creative streak, while a shorter one might indicate a more logical and analytical mindset.

Shape: A straight ring finger suggests clarity in creative expression, whereas a bent one might hint at unconventional tastes.

Little Finger (Mercury Finger)

Representing Mercury, the messenger god, the little finger delves into communication, intuition, and interpersonal connections.

Length: A long little finger is indicative of a skilled communicator, while a shorter one suggests a person who is more reticent in their expressions.

Shape: A straight little finger points to clear communication, but a bent one might indicate a more diplomatic or guarded nature.

The fingers, in their varied lengths and shapes, offer a wealth of information about an individual's character. While the lines and mounts on the palm provide insights into destiny and potential, the fingers highlight innate traits and tendencies. As always, in palmistry, it's vital to consider these interpretations as guiding insights, understanding that every hand tells a unique story, shaped by both destiny and choice.

The Significance of Finger Spacing and Flexibility in Palm Reading

Palmistry, with its roots tracing back to ancient civilizations, offers a unique lens through which we can gain insights into an individual's character and life path. While the lines and shapes of the hand often take center stage in palm readings, the spacing and flexibility of the fingers play a crucial role in understanding deeper nuances of one's personality.

Finger Spacing: A Reflection of Personal Boundaries and Social Dynamics

The spaces between the fingers can reveal a lot about how an individual interacts with the world and perceives their personal boundaries.

Individuals with wide spaces between their fingers often value independence and freedom. They are typically seen as open-minded, cherishing their personal space, and are not easily swayed by the opinions of the masses. Their approach to life is characterized by a willingness to explore diverse perspectives and experiences.

On the other hand, those with fingers closely set or with minimal spacing tend to be more introspective and cautious. They might hold their cards close to their chest, being selective about whom they share their innermost thoughts with. Such individuals often appreciate structure and might be more methodical in their approach to life.

The spacing between specific fingers also offers insights. For example, a noticeable gap between the middle and ring finger might suggest someone who likes to keep their professional and personal lives distinct and separate.

Finger Flexibility: Gauging Adaptability and Resilience

The degree to which fingers bend or resist bending can offer insights into an individual's adaptability and their response to challenges.

People with notably flexible fingers are often seen as adaptable and versatile. Life's twists and turns don't easily deter them. They are open to change and can navigate unexpected situations with grace and poise. Emotionally, such individuals might be more attuned to the feelings of others, showcasing empathy and understanding.

Conversely, those with stiffer fingers might be more set in their ways. They have a strong sense of their beliefs and might be less open to changing their viewpoints. While they can be seen as steadfast and reliable, they might also struggle when faced with situations that demand flexibility.

The flexibility of specific fingers can also be telling. For instance, a particularly flexible thumb might suggest someone who is adaptable in decision-making, while a rigid thumb could indicate a more stubborn disposition.

Combining Insights from Spacing and Flexibility

When we consider finger spacing and flexibility together, we get a more rounded picture of an individual's character. Someone with wide-spaced, flexible fingers might be an independent, adaptable thinker. In contrast, an individual with closely set, rigid fingers might prefer stability, routine, and might be more resistant to change.

In wrapping up, it's clear that the hands offer a wealth of information, with each feature adding a layer of depth to the reading. The spacing and flexibility of the fingers, though subtle, provide valuable insights into one's social interactions, adaptability, and overall approach to life. As always, it's essential to remember that while palmistry offers guidelines, the true essence of an individual is shaped by a myriad of factors, both inherent and chosen.

Fingerprints and Their Unique Interpretations in Palmistry

Fingerprints, with their intricate swirls and patterns, are a marvel of nature. Each individual possesses a unique set of fingerprints, making them a perfect tool for identification in forensic science. However, in the world of palmistry, these patterns take on a deeper, more symbolic meaning. They offer insights into an individual's character, tendencies, and even potential life paths.

The Basics of Fingerprints in Palmistry

Traditionally, palmistry has focused on the lines, mounts, and shapes of the hand. However, as our understanding of fingerprints has grown, so has their significance in palm readings. Each type of fingerprint pattern, be it a loop, whorl, or arch, is believed to correspond to specific personality traits and tendencies.

Types of Fingerprints and Their Interpretations

Loops are the most prevalent fingerprint pattern. These patterns are characterized by ridges that curve back on themselves. In the realm of palmistry, loops are symbolic of adaptability and flexibility. Individuals with predominant loop patterns on their fingertips are often seen as open to change and can easily adapt to new situations. Their nature is generally receptive, and they often have an innate ability to understand and resonate with others.

Whorls, with their circular or spiral patterns, are the next most common type of fingerprint. These patterns suggest individuals with a pronounced sense of self and independence. Those with whorl patterns often march to the beat of their own drum, possessing a clear sense of their desires and ambitions. They might be introspective and are often perceived as having a layered or complex personality.

Arches are straightforward patterns where the ridges rise in the center, forming a gentle arc. They are less common compared to loops and whorls. In palmistry, arches are indicative of practicality and a grounded nature. Individuals with arch patterns value stability and often prefer routines. They are seen as reliable and might be resistant to sudden changes or unpredictability.

Tented arches, a variation of the arch pattern, have a more pronounced and sharper rise in the center. This pattern is a blend of the practical nature of arches and the complexity associated with whorls. Individuals with tented arches might have a practical approach to life but can occasionally display intense passion or unpredictability.

Interpreting Fingerprints Alongside Other Hand Features

While fingerprints provide a wealth of information, it's essential to interpret them alongside other features of the hand for a holistic understanding. For instance, an individual with a loop fingerprint and a long Mercury finger might be adaptable and also possess strong communication skills. On the other hand, someone with a whorl pattern and a pronounced Mount of Venus might be independent and have a deep sense of passion.

The Modern Evolution of Fingerprints in Palmistry

It's interesting to note that the emphasis on fingerprints in palmistry is a more modern development. While traditional palmistry was centered around the lines and mounts of the hand, the significance of fingerprints has grown as our understanding of them has evolved in other fields, especially forensic science. Today, many palmists integrate fingerprint analysis into their readings, valuing the nuanced insights they bring to the table.

In conclusion, fingerprints, with their unique patterns, offer an added dimension to palm readings. They serve as subtle yet powerful indicators of an individual's inherent traits, complementing the insights from other features of the hand. As always, it's crucial to remember that while palmistry provides guidelines and insights, the true essence of an individual is a blend of nature, nurture, choices, and experiences.

CASE STUDY: MARIE, GRAND DUCHESS OF RUSSIA

Grand Duchess Maria Pavlovna of Russia, known as Maria Pavlovna the Younger (April 1890 – 13 December 1958), was a granddaughter of Alexander II of Russia. She was a paternal first cousin of Nicholas II, Russia's last Tsar, and a maternal first cousin of Prince Philip, Duke of Edinburgh, consort of Elizabeth II. She also held the distinction of being the first grandchild of George I of Greece and the first great-grandchild of Christian IX of Denmark.

Her early life was overshadowed by her mother's death and her father's banishment from Russia in 1902 after remarrying a commoner. Maria and her younger brother Dmitri, with whom she shared a lifelong close bond, were raised in Moscow by their paternal uncle, Grand Duke Sergei Alexandrovich, and his wife, Grand Duchess Elizabeth Feodorovna of Russia, a granddaughter of Queen Victoria.

In 1908, Maria Pavlovna married Prince Wilhelm, Duke of Södermanland, and they had one son, Prince Lennart, Duke of Småland, later Count Bernadotte af Wisborg. The marriage was troubled and ended in divorce in 1914. During World War I, she served as a nurse until the Russian monarchy fell in February 1917.

In September 1917, during the Russian Provisional Government, she married Prince Sergei Putyatin, with whom she had a son, Prince Roman Sergeievich Putyatin, who died in infancy. The couple fled revolutionary Russia through Ukraine in July 1918.

In exile, Maria Pavlovna briefly lived in Bucharest and London before settling in Paris in 1920. During the 1920s, she opened Kitmir, an embroidery fashion atelier, which enjoyed some success. She divorced her second husband in 1923 and, after selling Kitmir in 1928, emigrated to the United States. Residing in New York City, she published two memoirs: "The Education of a Princess" (1930) and "A Princess in Exile" (1932).

In 1942, she relocated to Argentina, where she spent the World War II years. She returned to Europe permanently in 1949 and passed away in Konstanz, Germany, in 1958.

Adapted from the character sketch from impressions of the hands of Grand Duchess, Marie July 6th, 1933 by Nellie Simmons Meier

Having previously taken impressions of the hands of H.I.ll., The Grand Duke Alexander, on July 6th, 1933, NSM had the opportunity to make impressions of the hands of H.I.H., the Grand Duchess Marie. This was made possible through one of her "roving lions," and she was delighted to welcome her to take these impressions, and spend time reading them.

NSM was eager to have those of Grand Duchess Marie. These individuals, who had inherited power and wealth for generations, fascinated her with their resilience in facing personal tragedies, the loss of their past glory, wealth, and status, and their ability to adapt to various forms of labor, from intellectual and artistic to menial.

Before meeting Grand Duchess Marie, NSM had heard that she possessed hands of exceptional beauty, rarely seen outside of works of art. However, her firm handshake surprised, conveying perfect mental and physical poise, a trait honed by necessity and tragic personal experiences.

The curve toward the base of her palm was a characteristic trait of the Russian people, reflecting a natural appreciation for art and beauty in all creative forms. The breadth of her palm under her fingers indicated a love of outdoor life, while the smooth, satiny skin with delicate capillary tracings suggested a preference for comfort over physical exertion.

Her right thumb was more flexible than her left, showing her acquired ability to mix with diverse people and endure uncomfortable or disagreeable surroundings with apparent ease. Despite her natural aloofness, indicated by the stiffness of her left thumb, and her inborn pride and love of power, shown in the high mount of Jupiter, this flexibility suggested she had adapted well to life's challenges. Her intuition, marked by the whorl on the mount of the Moon, aided her in this adaptation.

The drooping headline in both hands, coupled with her finely grained skin, indicated a mind sensitive to life's experiences, absorbing and reflecting them to gain strength and knowledge. Her intellectual response to life's highs and lows was like a lithographing stone, capable of capturing varied hues and details, then wiping clean for the next experience. This mental resilience was akin to the defenders of Verdun's motto, "On ne passera pas."

Her logical and reasoning powers, denoted by the length of the second phalanges of her thumbs, helped her navigate the complexities of mental and social readjustment. Her long fourth finger, indicating diplomacy, further aided her in these endeavors.

Her first finger's length revealed her natural leadership abilities and desire for power. She used her quick perceptions, shown by the pointed tips of her first fingers, to face and master life's varied challenges.

The long first phalange of her second finger, with its rounded tip, displayed an innate buoyancy and a mindset that things could always be worse, helping her overcome life's obstacles.

The forked head line in her right hand, indicating intellectual brilliance, and her gift of expression, helped her overcome barriers and find safe paths to her goals. However, the length of the middle phalange of her second finger, indicating prudence, was an obstacle to her over-caution, as shown in the close joining of the life and head lines in her left hand.

Her smooth fingers, along with the stretch between her third and fourth fingers, indicated quick thought and action, helping her overcome tendencies to wait for events to happen.

The length of her third finger's first phalange showed her love for idealism in art, with a keen ability to detect flaws. Her love of color, indicated by the middle phalange, was tempered by caution and conservatism, shown in the joining of the life and head lines in her left hand.

The flare of her little finger from the hand, coupled with the power of words shown in the tip, indicated a love for the dramatic side of life and a preference for rapid events over dwelling on tragic shadows.

A notable mark in her right hand was the well-defined lines of ability on the mount under the third finger. Necessity had forced her to turn her artistic desires into practical use, earning recognition in literature and personal enterprise. Her courage, never recognizing defeat and covered with the velvet gauntlet of diplomacy, perseverance, and intellectual brilliance, was guided wisely in using the necessary tools for success.

Grand Bechun Marie
July 6th 1933

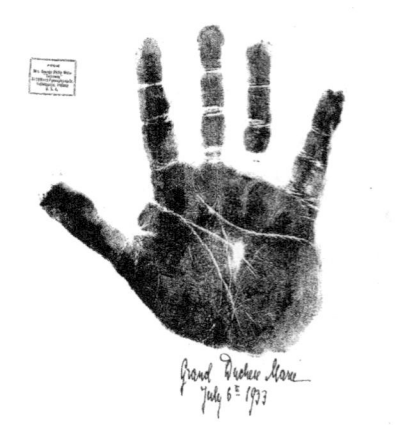

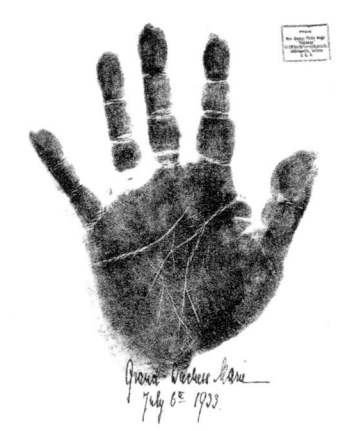

Grand Bechun Marie
July 6th 1933

CHAPTER 9

Special Markings and Symbols

Special Markings and Symbols in Palmistry

Palmistry, with its roots deep in ancient cultures, offers a window into the soul through the lines and shapes of the hand. While the primary lines, such as the heart, head, and life lines, often capture the spotlight in palm readings, there's a world of intricate markings and symbols that hold their own tales. These special markings, ranging from crosses to chains, provide additional insights into an individual's life, challenges, and potential.

Crosses are intersecting lines that form a shape reminiscent of a cross. Their significance in a reading largely depends on their location. Generally, crosses can indicate challenges or pivotal moments in one's life. For instance, a cross situated on the Mount of Jupiter might hint at challenges related to leadership or a crucial decision that affects one's ambitions.

Stars, formed by three or more lines intersecting at a central point, are often seen as auspicious signs. They typically indicate moments of success, enlightenment, or unexpected good fortune. The specific interpretation, however, is tied to its location. A star on the Mount of Apollo, for example, could signify a burst of fame or a significant achievement in the arts.

Islands, appearing as elongated oval shapes along a line, often suggest interruptions or disruptions. They can be indicative of stress, health issues, or periods of uncertainty. Their meaning is closely associated with the line they appear on. An island on the Heart Line, for instance, might point to emotional challenges or a turbulent phase in a relationship.

Chains, characterized by a series of interconnected circles along a line, often denote feelings of being trapped in repetitive patterns or periods of indecision. The line on which they appear provides context to their meaning. Chains on the Head Line might suggest mental confusion or a phase of indecisiveness.

Grilles, with their grid-like pattern formed by intersecting lines, suggest a scattering or dissipation of energy. When found on a mount, they might indicate that the energies associated with that mount are not being fully harnessed. For instance, a grille on the Mount of Mercury could hint at challenges in effective communication or a tendency to have scattered thoughts.

Triangles, formed by three intersecting lines, are generally seen as positive symbols in palmistry. They might indicate a balanced perspective or even protection against challenges. Their specific meaning is tied to their location. A triangle on the Mount of Saturn might suggest a harmonious balance between introspection and worldly interactions.

Squares, with their four-sided shape, are protective symbols. They often indicate a safeguarding force during challenging times. For example, a square that appears around an island might suggest protection or a buffer during a challenging period.

Dots, small and round, can be found on lines or mounts. They often signify significant events, moments of crisis, or sudden realizations. Their interpretation is closely linked to where they appear. A dot on the Life Line, for instance, could indicate a transformative event or a significant turning point in one's life.

In essence, the hand in palmistry is a detailed map of an individual's life journey. Each marking, with its unique significance tied to its location, offers insights into specific events, tendencies, and characteristics. By delving into the relationship between markings and their positions, palmists can weave together the intricate tapestry of an individual's life, guiding them through past experiences, present challenges, and potential future paths.

The world of palmistry is rich and varied. Beyond the primary lines lie a plethora of symbols and markings, each holding its secrets and stories. These special markings add depth and nuance to a palm reading, offering a more detailed and comprehensive view of an individual's life journey. As always, it's essential to approach these symbols with an understanding that they provide insights and possibilities, not definitive outcomes. The true journey of an individual is a blend of fate, choices, experiences, and the myriad symbols that grace their hand.

Interpreting Symbols in a Palmistry Reading

Palmistry is a delicate art that delves into the intricate patterns and symbols of the hand to reveal insights about an individual's life and destiny. While understanding the fundamental meanings of these symbols is crucial, the real mastery lies in interpreting them in the context of a comprehensive reading. Here's a deeper look into how to interpret these symbols effectively.

Start by observing the overall hand. Before diving deep into specific symbols, it's essential to get a general feel of the hand. The hand's shape, texture, and even its color can provide foundational insights that set the tone for the reading.

Context plays a pivotal role. The meaning of a symbol can change dramatically based on its location on the hand. For instance, a star on the Mount of Apollo has different implications than one found on the Heart Line. It's always important to consider the broader context of the symbol's location and the primary attributes of that area.

Symbols often interact with each other. It's rare for a symbol to operate in isolation. Combinations of symbols can offer more nuanced insights. For example, a triangle on the Life Line might suggest protection, but if it's near a square, the interpretation could lean towards protection during a challenging period.

The clarity and size of symbols are significant. A symbol that's distinct and clear might indicate a more pronounced event or characteristic in an individual's life compared to a symbol that's faint or blurred.

Consider the life stage of the individual. The personal context of the individual being read is crucial. For example, certain symbols on a younger person's hand might relate to potential future events, while on an older individual's hand, they might pertain to past experiences.

Trust your intuition. While there are traditional interpretations for symbols, sometimes a symbol might evoke a specific feeling or insight that's unique to the reading. Intuition can often lead to deeper, more personalized insights.

Engage in a dialogue. A palmistry session is as much about listening as it is about interpreting. Engaging with the person being read, asking open-ended questions, and considering their feedback can provide valuable context to the reading.

Life is dynamic, and so are our hands. It's essential to remember that hands change over time, reflecting the ever-evolving nature of our lives. Some symbols might indicate future potentials, while others might reflect past experiences.

Stay updated and keep learning. The field of palmistry is vast and ever-evolving. Regularly updating one's knowledge and being open to different interpretations can enhance the depth and accuracy of readings.

Lastly, approach readings with empathy and ethical responsibility. It's essential to provide insights in a manner that's empowering, avoiding any interpretations that might instill undue fear or anxiety.

In essence, interpreting symbols in palmistry is a blend of skill, intuition, and empathy. Each hand offers a unique story, and each symbol is a piece of that narrative puzzle. By approaching readings with a holistic perspective and a keen understanding of symbols and their context, palmists can offer valuable insights that resonate deeply with those seeking guidance.

CASE STUDY: BOOKER T. WASHINGTON

Adapted from the character sketch from impressions of the hands of Booker T. Washington on by Nellie Simmons Meier

NSM met Booker T. Washington in June 1903 when he visited Indianapolis to speak about his Tuskegee Normal and Industrial Institute of Alabama. During his stay, a notable incident occurred at the Hotel English, where the Negro waiters threatened to strike if asked to serve him. Fortunately, prominent white professionals and businessmen intervened, ensuring Washington was well-received.

NSM was particularly intrigued by Washington's hands, which strikingly resembled those of John Mitchell, the first president of the United Mine Workers of America. This similarity was noteworthy, as President Theodore Roosevelt, known for seeking firsthand information, had also hosted Mitchell. Roosevelt's invitation to Washington to lunch at the White House exemplified that trait of President Roosevelt's character, his determination to gain his information from the original source rather than from hearsay.

Washington's hands, with their breadth under the fingers curving toward the wrist, suggested a practical approach to life combined with lofty aspirations. His well-placed, stiff thumbs indicated a tenacious resolve, undeterred by obstacles, supported by reason and logic. His ability to concentrate efforts was evident in the stiffness of his thumbs, leading to lasting achievements. The breadth of his palm suggested a constitution suited to outdoor life, while his smooth fingers indicated quick decision-making abilities and a balance to his cautious nature.

The balanced phalanges of his fingers pointed to a guiding conscience, reasoned intellect, and a practical foundation essential for progress. Washington's practical understanding of money, his planning skills, and quick decision-making, coupled with his conscience, earned him the confidence of both the highly intelligent and the less informed. His optimistic nature, indicated by the pointed tip of his middle finger, inspired hope in adverse conditions.

The developed appreciation for creative art in Washington's third finger, with an eye for quality and workmanship, showed his practical yet idealistic approach. His fourth fingers revealed his tact in management and his expressive gift, making him a leader who led by example and reached people with heartfelt words based on personal belief and experience.

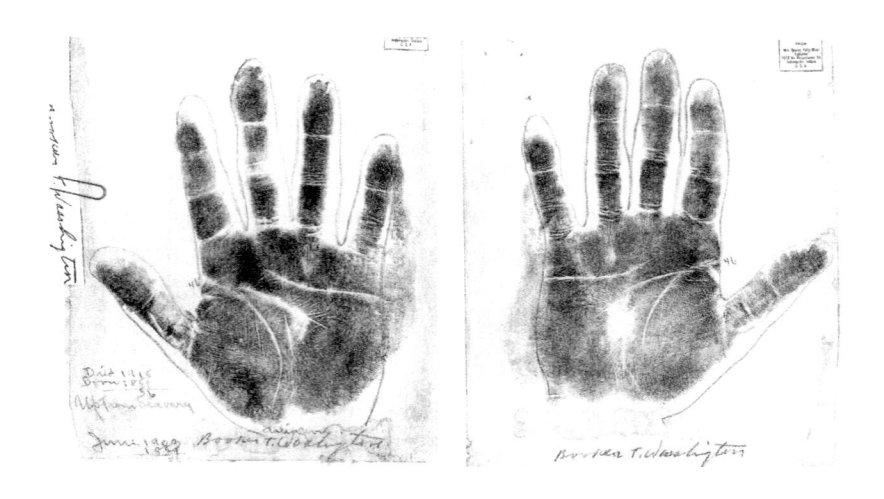

CHAPTER 10

Putting It All Together

Applying Palmistry in Everyday Life: Using Palmistry as a Tool for Personal Growth and Understanding

Palmistry, the ancient art of reading the lines and features of the hand, is not merely a form of entertainment or fortune-telling. It is a profound tool for self-discovery and personal growth, offering valuable insights into our inner selves and helping us navigate life's complexities with greater understanding and awareness. In this chapter, we explore how we can apply palmistry in our everyday lives to gain a deeper understanding of ourselves, foster personal growth, and enhance our relationships with others.

The Role of Palmistry in Self-Reflection

In a fast-paced world filled with endless distractions, finding moments of self-reflection can be challenging. Palmistry provides a tangible and accessible way to connect with ourselves and delve into our subconscious thoughts, emotions, and desires. The lines, mounts, and features of our hands serve as a mirror reflecting our unique personalities, strengths, and challenges. By incorporating palmistry into our daily routines, we create opportunities for introspection and self-awareness.

Embracing Self-Awareness

One of the primary benefits of applying palmistry in everyday life is the cultivation of self-awareness. Through the exploration of our own hand, we gain insights into our emotional nature, thought patterns, and life experiences. The heart line reveals our approach to love and relationships, the head line showcases our communication style and intellectual pursuits, and the life line offers clues about our vitality and resilience.

As we embrace the revelations from palmistry, we become more conscious of our tendencies and reactions, empowering us to make informed choices aligned with our truest selves. With this self-awareness, we can navigate life's challenges with greater wisdom and adaptability.

Making Informed Decisions

Incorporating palmistry into our daily lives also enhances our decision-making process. By understanding our strengths and weaknesses, we can identify areas where we excel and where we may need additional support or growth. For example, someone with a strong mount of Mercury may have excellent communication skills and analytical abilities, making them well-suited for careers that involve problem-solving and strategizing.

On the other hand, recognizing a less prominent mount of Venus may indicate a need to prioritize self-care and emotional well-being. Armed with this knowledge, we can make conscious choices about career paths, relationships, and lifestyle changes that align with our natural inclinations and aspirations.

Navigating Relationships

Palmistry can also play a valuable role in understanding our relationships with others. By analyzing our hands alongside the hands of our loved ones, we gain insights into compatibility, communication styles, and potential areas of growth within the relationship. Recognizing the strengths and challenges in our connections can facilitate open and constructive communication, fostering deeper intimacy and understanding.

For instance, if one partner has a strong heart line, indicating a more emotionally expressive nature, and the other has a more reserved heart line, understanding these differences can lead to greater empathy and appreciation for each other's unique ways of relating.

Cultivating Empathy and Compassion

As we explore the intricacies of our own hands, we develop a greater appreciation for the diversity of human experience. Palmistry teaches us that each individual is a complex tapestry of qualities, potentials, and life experiences. This understanding fosters empathy and compassion, enabling us to connect with others on a deeper level and embrace their uniqueness without judgment.

Setting Personal Goals

Incorporating palmistry into our everyday lives can also inspire us to set personal goals for growth and development. For example, if we notice a fragmented head line, which may suggest a tendency to overthink and worry, we can consciously work on cultivating mindfulness and stress-reducing practices.

Likewise, recognizing a strong mount of Jupiter, indicative of leadership abilities and a desire for growth, can encourage us to pursue opportunities for career advancement or personal development. Palmistry becomes a roadmap for personal evolution, empowering us to take charge of our lives and set intentions for positive change.

Embracing Personal Growth

Palmistry is a powerful catalyst for personal growth and transformation. As we engage with the messages and symbols within our hands, we become aware of patterns that may be holding us back from reaching our fullest potential. Through self-reflection and self-analysis, we can address limiting beliefs, heal emotional wounds, and let go of self-imposed restrictions.

By embracing personal growth, we open ourselves to new possibilities and opportunities for fulfillment. The lines on our palms may evolve over time as we navigate life's ups and downs, reflecting our growth and evolution as individuals.

Integrating Palmistry into Daily Rituals

To apply palmistry in everyday life, consider incorporating it into your daily rituals. Set aside a few moments each day for self-palm reading, journaling your observations, and reflecting on the insights gained. Establishing a routine creates a sacred space for introspection, self-awareness, and personal growth.

The Power of Self-Discovery through Palmistry

In conclusion, applying palmistry in our everyday lives offers a wealth of opportunities for personal growth and understanding. By embracing self-awareness, making informed decisions, navigating relationships, cultivating empathy, setting personal goals, and embracing personal growth, we empower ourselves to lead more fulfilling and purposeful lives.

Palmistry serves as a mirror reflecting the essence of who we are and the potential of who we can become. As we unlock the mysteries within our hands, we gain a deeper appreciation for our uniqueness and the richness of the human experience. Through the integration of palmistry into our daily routines, we embark on a transformative journey of self-discovery and self-empowerment, aligning with our truest selves and embracing the beauty of our individuality. As we continue to explore the art of palmistry, let us celebrate the profound connection between palmistry and self-awareness, recognizing that the path of self-discovery lies right at the tips of our fingers.

Case Studies and Examples of Palm Readings

In this chapter, we delve into the fascinating world of example palm readings, exploring detailed case studies that illustrate the art and science of palmistry in action. Each palm reading serves as a captivating example of how the lines, mounts, and features of the hand can reveal unique insights into an individual's personality, life experiences, and potential paths.

1. Case Study: The Artist's Journey

Subject: Emily W.

Emily W., a 32-year-old artist, sought a palm reading with the goal of gaining clarity about her life purpose and creative potential. Her hands presented a myriad of fascinating features that shed light on her artistic journey.

Dominant Hand Right Hand

Emily's right hand showcased a prominent and creative Apollo (Sun) mount, signifying a natural flair for artistic expression and a strong desire to make a lasting impact through her work. The Apollo mount's shape and firmness indicated her disciplined and determined approach to her craft.

Her head line gently curved upwards, suggesting a balanced combination of creativity and practicality. This trait allowed her to infuse her artistic endeavors with a touch of pragmatism, making her artwork both imaginative and commercially viable.

The heart line revealed her emotional depth and sensitivity. Its gentle curve and depth indicated her profound emotional connections with her art, and her empathetic nature toward her audience.

Emily's life line, surprisingly short, portrayed her fearless spirit and willingness to take risks in pursuit of her creative passions. This trait also indicated that she had a deep appreciation for living in the present moment, rather than being overly concerned about the future.

Non-Dominant Hand Left Hand

Emily's left hand showcased a more developed Mercury (Little) finger, indicating her strong communication skills and her ability to articulate her artistic vision effectively. This attribute was essential in networking with fellow artists, gallery owners, and potential clients.

Her fate line, starting prominently at the base of her palm, portrayed her determination to forge her path as an artist. Its unbroken trajectory and slight curvature towards the Saturn mount revealed a steady, long-term commitment to her artistic pursuits.

Overall, Emily's hands revealed a passionate and dedicated artist, eager to leave her mark on the world through her creative expression. The reading provided her with the reassurance that she was indeed on the right path and encouraged her to continue honing her skills and exploring various mediums to fully realize her artistic potential.

2. Case Study: The Business Leader's Destiny

Subject: John D.

John D., a 45-year-old business executive, sought a palm reading to gain insight into his career and life direction. His hands presented a unique combination of features that hinted at his leadership potential and innate business acumen.

Dominant Hand Right Hand

John's right hand showcased a well-defined Jupiter (Index) finger, signifying his leadership qualities, ambition, and desire for success. The length and shape of the Jupiter finger indicated his natural inclination to take charge and inspire others.

His head line, with a strong and straightforward trajectory, portrayed his practical and logical approach to problem-solving. This trait served him well in making sound business decisions and navigating complex challenges.

The heart line demonstrated his caring and compassionate nature, hinting at his ability to form meaningful connections with colleagues and subordinates. This emotional intelligence played a crucial role in motivating and fostering a harmonious work environment.

John's life line exhibited a long and distinct line, stretching across the palm. This signified his endurance and resilience in the face of adversity, providing him with the determination to overcome obstacles and achieve his goals.

Non-Dominant Hand Left Hand

John's left hand revealed a balanced and prominent Mercury (Little) finger, signifying his effective communication skills and persuasive abilities. This attribute proved valuable in negotiations, presentations, and networking within the business world.

His fate line was well-defined and started close to the life line, indicating that his career path was closely linked to his personal life and upbringing. The fate line's clear trajectory towards the Saturn mount portrayed his strong sense of responsibility and discipline.

Overall, John's hands revealed a born leader with a powerful sense of purpose and direction. The reading provided him with valuable insights into his innate leadership qualities and encouraged him to continue pursuing his professional goals with determination and vision.

3. Case Study: The Healer's Calling

Subject: Sarah M.

Sarah M., a 29-year-old nurse, sought a palm reading to gain clarity about her career and spiritual journey. Her hands presented a unique blend of features that hinted at her compassionate and nurturing nature.

Dominant Hand Right Hand

Sarah's right hand showcased a prominent and rounded Moon mount, signifying her strong empathetic abilities and deep intuition. This feature pointed to her natural inclination to care for others and provide emotional support.

Her head line, gently curving downwards, indicated her sensitive and compassionate approach to problem-solving. This trait allowed her to connect with patients on a profound level, making her a respected and beloved healthcare professional.

The heart line demonstrated her nurturing and caring nature, reflecting her commitment to healing and tending to the emotional needs of her patients. Its curvature towards the Jupiter mount hinted at her strong sense of duty and dedication to her profession.

Sarah's life line, slightly curved and well-defined, indicated her grounded and stable nature. Her sense of responsibility and caring extended beyond her professional life and encompassed her personal relationships as well.

Non-Dominant Hand Left Hand

Sarah's left hand revealed a well-balanced and proportionate Mercury (Little) finger, suggesting her effective communication skills and ability to connect with others through her words. This attribute proved invaluable in conveying information to patients and collaborating with medical teams.

Her fate line was well-defined and gracefully curved towards the Apollo mount, indicating a fulfilling and purposeful career in healthcare. The fate line's trajectory suggested a strong alignment with her inner calling.

Overall, Sarah's hands revealed a caring and empathetic healer, destined to make a significant impact in the lives of her patients. The reading provided her with the reassurance that her career path was indeed aligned with her true calling, encouraging her to continue providing compassionate care to those in need.

Insights from Example Palm Readings

The case studies presented in this chapter offer a glimpse into the transformative power of palmistry. Each palm reading illustrates the intricate connection between the lines, mounts, and features of the hand and the unique qualities and potential of the individual. From artists to business leaders and healers, palmistry offers valuable insights that resonate deeply with each person's life journey.

It is essential to note that palmistry is not a deterministic tool, but rather a guiding compass that empowers individuals to embrace their strengths, address their challenges, and embark on paths of personal growth and fulfillment. Each palm reading serves as a reminder that we are the architects of our destinies, and palmistry provides us with valuable insights to make informed decisions and create meaningful lives.

As we continue to explore the world of palmistry, let these real-life case studies inspire us to delve into the rich tapestry of our own hands and unlock the mysteries that lie within. By embracing the wisdom and guidance of palmistry, we embark on a profound journey of self-discovery, self-awareness, and personal growth, enriching our lives and the lives of those around us.

Handprints and Illustrations: Visual Aids for Better Understanding

In the fascinating world of palmistry, handprints and illustrations play a crucial role in enhancing our understanding of the intricate lines, mounts, and features of the hand. As we embark on a journey to explore the art and science of palmistry, these visual aids provide valuable insights that complement textual descriptions and offer a more comprehensive view of the unique patterns and characteristics present in each individual's hand.

The Power of Handprints: Unveiling Individuality

Handprints are a powerful tool in palmistry, allowing us to capture and preserve the unique imprints of an individual's hand. Unlike traditional ink prints, modern technology allows us to create digital handprints that can be magnified, analyzed, and compared with precision. Each handprint acts as a personal signature, unveiling the individuality and complexity of the hand's lines and mounts.

Through handprints, palmists can conduct more in-depth analyses and identify subtle variations in the lines, such as breaks, forks, islands, or crosses. These intricacies can carry significant meaning and reveal insights into an individual's character, emotional tendencies, and life experiences.

Handprints also serve as valuable tools for tracking changes over time. By comparing handprints taken at different stages of life, palmists can observe how the lines and features evolve, reflecting the impact of experiences and personal growth.

Handprint Analysis: Key Considerations

As a helpful reminder, when analyzing handprints, palmists take into account various factors that contribute to the overall reading. These considerations include:

Hand Shape

The hand's shape provides valuable information about an individual's temperament and personality traits. There are four main hand shapes: earth, air, fire, and water. An earth hand is characterized by a square palm and short fingers, indicating practicality and stability. An air hand features a rectangular palm and long fingers, suggesting intellect and curiosity. A fire hand is distinguished by a rectangular palm and short fingers, symbolizing enthusiasm and passion. A water hand exhibits an oval palm and long, slender fingers, reflecting sensitivity and creativity.

Finger Proportions

The proportions of the fingers offer insights into an individual's communication style and intellectual tendencies. The length of the fingers in relation to each other can indicate qualities such as assertiveness, intuition, practicality, and creativity.

Mounts

Mounts are fleshy areas on the palm that correspond to specific planets and carry unique qualities. The size, shape, and prominence of these mounts reveal various aspects of an individual's personality and strengths. For example, a well-developed Jupiter mount indicates leadership abilities, while a strong Venus mount suggests a love for art and beauty.

Major Lines

The major lines on the palm include the heart line, head line, life line, and fate line. Each line represents different aspects of an individual's life, such as emotions, intellect, vitality, and destiny. The depth, length, and curvature of these lines convey essential information about one's emotional stability, mental focus, physical well-being, and life path.

Minor Lines

In addition to the major lines, palmists examine the minor lines, such as the health line, marriage line, and money line. These lines provide supplementary details that enrich the overall palm reading. For instance, the money line reveals insights into financial prospects, while the marriage line offers glimpses into one's relationships and partnerships.

CASE STUDY: SUSAN B. ANTHONY

Susan B. Anthony

Susan B. Anthony (1820-1906) was a pioneering figure in the American women's suffrage movement, dedicating her life to the fight for equal rights for women. Born on February 15, 1820, in Adams, Massachusetts, Anthony grew up in a Quaker family known for their commitment to social equality. Her upbringing instilled in her a strong sense of justice and activism.

In her early years, Anthony was involved in the anti-slavery movement. However, her focus shifted predominantly to women's rights after she met fellow activist Elizabeth Cady Stanton in 1851. Together, they formed a lifelong partnership in activism. Anthony played a crucial role in various campaigns for women's rights, including property rights, labor rights, and the right to vote.

One of her most significant contributions was co-founding the National Woman Suffrage Association in 1869 with Stanton. This organization played a pivotal role in advocating for women's voting rights. Anthony's dedication to the cause led to her arrest in 1872 for illegally voting in the presidential election, an event that brought significant attention to the suffrage movement.

Anthony tirelessly traveled across the United States and Europe, giving speeches and organizing events to garner support for women's suffrage. Her ability to strategize, organize, and mobilize made her an effective leader in the movement. She also played a key role in the creation of The Revolution, a weekly publication dedicated to women's rights.

Despite facing considerable opposition and challenges, Anthony remained steadfast in her pursuit of equal rights for women. She did not live to see the fruition of her efforts; however, her relentless advocacy laid the groundwork for the eventual ratification of the 19th Amendment in 1920, granting women the right to vote.

Susan B. Anthony passed away on March 13, 1906, but her legacy as a trailblazer in the fight for women's suffrage and equality continues to inspire generations. Her life's work is a testament to the power of perseverance and dedication in the pursuit of social justice.

Adapted from the character sketch from impressions of the hands of Susan B. Anthony by Nellie Simmons Meier

We present the hand of the late Susan B. Anthony, a Suffrage Pioneer and contemporary of Jane Addams. Anthony's lifelong dedication to women's suffrage remains an enduring testament to her efforts. Like Addams, whose work significantly improved everyday life conditions, Anthony's impact is lasting. NSM met her in December 1899, hosted by NSM's former teacher May Wright Sewell, a renowned advocate for women's causes. The hands of Anthony and Addams appeared strikingly similar, reflecting their shared humanitarian mission.

Anthony's hand was square with a spatulate tendency, suggesting a practical, methodical nature committed to law and order, combined with a restless drive for action. Her long fingers indicated meticulous attention to detail in all aspects, from dress to business and public speaking, with no room for superficiality or shortcuts.

The developed joints in her hands signified a desire for material order, while her headline suggested this extended to her mental and practical realms. The firmness of her palm indicated her capacity to create order from chaos through physical and mental efforts. Surprisingly, her pointed fingertips revealed an artistic side, subordinate to her practical nature.

Her willpower, evident in the length of her thumb's first phalange, was balanced by the logic shown in the second phalange. Her beliefs and actions were grounded in facts and reason, not impulse. The stiffness of her thumbs and the thinness of the nail phalanges highlighted her executive abilities and quick perception, enabling her to identify and exploit her opponents' weaknesses.

The length and shape of her second finger, Saturn, revealed her need for periodic retreats to rejuvenate spiritually, mentally, and physically. The slightly pointed tip reflected her ability to overcome the challenges faced by suffrage pioneers with optimism.

The middle phalange of her fingers indicated her love for knowledge with practical applications. Her third finger, Apollo, showed a reasoned love for art, indifferent to transient trends. The fourth finger, Mercury, revealed her tact in detail management, with the first phalange underscoring her conscientiousness. The pointed tip demonstrated her skill in clear, concise expression, even in spontaneous speech. Her philosophical joints suggested that her convictions were shaped by reason rather than emotion.

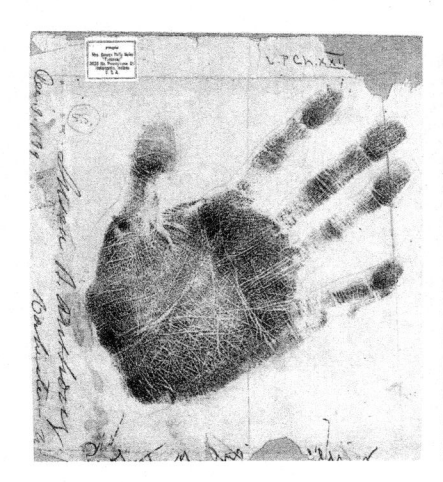

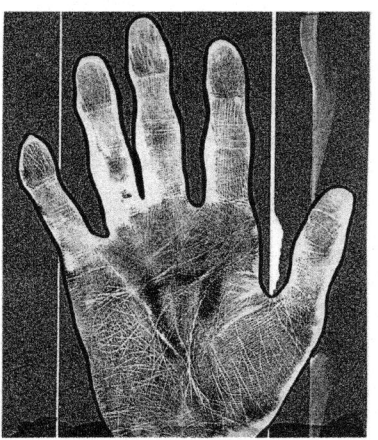

CHAPTER 11

Ethical Considerations in Palmistry

The Responsibilities of a Palm Reader in Palmistry

As we've covered, palmistry as an age-old practice, delves into the intricate lines and shapes of the hand to offer insights into an individual's character, destiny, and even past experiences. As intriguing as the art is, it comes with a weighty responsibility. A palm reader, often perceived as a conduit between the mystical realm and the tangible world, occupies a position of trust and influence. Their interpretations can mold perceptions, guide decisions, and even redirect life paths. Recognizing the responsibility of a palm reader is essential for both practitioners and seekers.

At the heart of a palm reader's duty lies a steadfast commitment to ethical integrity. Given the deeply personal nature of palmistry, a reader must approach each session with utmost honesty. It's imperative to resist the urge to exaggerate, invent, or offer misleading interpretations for personal advantage. Genuine and authentic readings not only maintain the dignity of the practice but also ensure that seekers receive true guidance.

Another crucial aspect is sensitivity and empathy. The hand can reveal moments of joy, challenges, achievements, and struggles. When interpreting these revelations, a palm reader must tread with care, understanding the emotional ramifications of their words.

Delivering insights, especially those that might be challenging, requires kindness and a compassionate touch.

Confidentiality is a cornerstone of the practice. When individuals offer their hands for reading, they are, in essence, sharing their life stories. This trust is sacred, and a palm reader must ensure that the insights from a reading remain private. Any breach of this trust not only tarnishes the reputation of the reader but also violates the intimate bond between the reader and the seeker.

While palmistry can hint at potential life events and paths, making absolute predictions is a pitfall to avoid. The future is a tapestry woven from individual choices, external events, and perhaps destiny. By presenting insights as fixed outcomes, a palm reader might inadvertently limit the individual's perception of their own agency. It's more prudent to present insights as potential paths, emphasizing personal choice and empowerment.

Continuous learning is integral to the practice. Palmistry is a vast field with evolving interpretations and diverse schools of thought. A dedicated palm reader is always on the path of learning, aiming to deepen their understanding and hone their skills. This commitment ensures that their readings remain informed and relevant.

It's also essential for palm readers to set clear boundaries. While palmistry can offer spiritual and emotional insights, it shouldn't replace professional advice in areas like health, finance, or legal matters. Recognizing and respecting the limits of their expertise is crucial.

Before embarking on a reading, managing the expectations of the seeker is vital. This involves clarifying what palmistry can and cannot offer and ensuring that the individual approaches the reading with an open and receptive mindset.

A palm reader's responsibility also encompasses their own well-being. Engaging deeply with others' energies and narratives can be emotionally draining. Regular self-care practices and grounding techniques are essential to ensure the reader remains balanced and can offer the best guidance.

The words used during a reading carry immense weight. A responsible palm reader is acutely aware of their choice of words, ensuring they empower, enlighten, and guide. Avoiding language that induces fear or dependence is crucial, given the lasting impact words can have.

Lastly, respecting the rich history and tradition of palmistry is fundamental. Palmistry has been practiced across cultures and epochs. Honoring its legacy and the wisdom of past practitioners ensures the art is practiced with the reverence it deserves.

The role of a palm reader is both influential and delicate. With the privilege of offering insights into an individual's life comes a profound responsibility. By practicing with integrity, empathy, and a commitment to continuous growth, palm readers can honor the tradition of palmistry while empowering individuals to chart their life's journey with clarity and confidence.

The Role and Duty of a Palm Reader

For ages, palmistry has delved into the intricate patterns of the hand, drawing from its lines, shapes, and mounts to understand an individual's nature, potential journeys, and even glimpses of their past and future. This age-old practice, revered across cultures, bestows upon the palm reader a profound duty. Positioned at the intersection of the ethereal and the tangible, a palm reader wields considerable influence. Their readings have the potential to mold beliefs, guide choices, and reshape destinies. Recognizing and honoring this duty is essential for both the practitioners of palmistry and those who turn to them for guidance.

Avoiding False Predictions and Managing Expectations

Predictions, whether in the realm of finance, weather forecasting, or personal guidance disciplines like astrology and palmistry, have always held a certain allure. They promise a glimpse into the future, based on patterns, data, or perceived signs. However, the act of predicting is fraught with complexities, given the myriad variables that influence outcomes. The responsibility that comes with making predictions is immense, and it's vital to tread with caution and integrity. Avoiding false predictions and effectively managing expectations is not just an ethical imperative but also crucial for maintaining trust and professional credibility.

The dangers of false predictions are manifold. Firstly, there's the immediate consequence of diminished credibility. Professionals who consistently offer inaccurate forecasts risk being viewed as unreliable or even untrustworthy. This loss of trust can be particularly damaging in fields where personal guidance is involved, as individuals often make significant life decisions based on these predictions.

Beyond credibility, the emotional and psychological impact of false predictions can be profound. Inaccurate forecasts, especially in personal guidance or therapeutic contexts, can lead to feelings of disappointment, heightened anxiety, or misplaced optimism. In more pragmatic sectors, like finance, the repercussions can be tangibly severe, leading to substantial monetary losses for those who acted based on inaccurate predictions.

So, how can one avoid making false predictions? Continuous learning and staying updated with the latest methodologies in one's field is paramount. This ensures that professionals are equipped with the most current tools and knowledge to make informed forecasts. Additionally, verifying the authenticity and timeliness of the data used for predictions is essential. Outdated or incorrect data can significantly skew outcomes.

Another strategy is to collaborate or seek second opinions. Different perspectives can offer a more holistic view and might highlight potential biases or oversights that one might miss. Most importantly, it's wise to avoid making predictions in absolutes. Given the inherent uncertainties of the future, offering a spectrum of possible outcomes, rather than a definitive prediction, is often more accurate and responsible.

Managing expectations is equally crucial. Clear and transparent communication about the basis of any prediction, the variables at play, and potential uncertainties can help set realistic expectations. Especially in fields of personal guidance, emphasizing the role of individual choice is vital. While predictions can offer a roadmap, it's the individual's actions and decisions that truly shape their path.

Providing regular updates or revised forecasts, especially in dynamic sectors, can also help in managing expectations. This not only acknowledges the evolving nature of data and circumstances but ensures that individuals or stakeholders have the most current information at their disposal.

Establishing a feedback mechanism is another effective strategy. Feedback from those who receive and act on predictions can offer invaluable insights into the accuracy and impact of forecasts. This feedback loop can be instrumental in refining future predictions and understanding how best to manage expectations.

The act of predicting, while powerful, is laden with responsibilities. Professionals must navigate this space with a blend of expertise, caution, and ethical consideration. By focusing on accuracy, transparency, and continuous learning, they can offer valuable insights while respecting the complexities and uncertainties inherent in predicting the future.

CASE STUDY: LESLIE HOWARD

Leslie Howard, an acclaimed English actor, was celebrated for his portrayal of intellectuals and gentlemen in a career spanning three decades. Born in London in 1893 to Lilian and Ferdinand "Frank" Steiner, he overcame a shy, sheltered childhood to pursue a career in the arts, despite his father's preference for a banking job. His acting career, which began as a therapeutic outlet after suffering shell shock in World War I, led to his film debut in "The Happy Warrior" (1917) and a successful stage career in London and on Broadway.

Howard co-founded Minerva Films in 1920, but after its quick bankruptcy, he achieved Broadway success, leading to his Hollywood debut in "Outward Bound" (1930). He starred in several 1930s hits, including "The Animal Kingdom," "Of Human Bondage" with Bette Davis, and iconic roles in "The Scarlet Pimpernel," "Pygmalion," and "Gone With the Wind."

Critical of Hollywood, Howard returned to England in 1940 to contribute to the war effort through propaganda films and broadcasting for the BBC. His life tragically ended at 50 when his plane was shot down by the German Luftwaffe in 1943, leading to speculation about his possible intelligence work. Remembered as a refined and sensitive actor, Howard's legacy continues as a symbol of British cinema's golden age.

We don't have the notes for Leslie Howard's palm reading by NSM so what do you see?

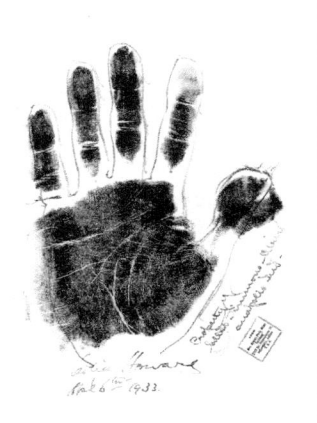

CHAPTER 12

Advanced Techniques and Further Study

Palmistry is a captivating discipline that provides insights into an individual's character, destiny, and potential through the study of the hand. While many are acquainted with its foundational concepts, such as interpreting the primary lines, there's a vast realm of advanced techniques waiting to be explored by those eager to deepen their understanding.

Dermatoglyphics, or the study of the intricate patterns of ridges on the fingers and palms, is one such advanced technique. Commonly recognized as fingerprints, these patterns are established during fetal development and remain consistent throughout life. They can offer a glimpse into an individual's inherent talents, potential health predispositions, and even behavioral tendencies. For instance, a whorl pattern on a fingertip might be indicative of a person with a sharp, analytical mind, while an arch pattern could suggest someone more grounded and practical.

Another fascinating area of study is the finger phalanges. Each finger is segmented into phalanges, and the relative lengths and shapes of these segments can reveal unique personality traits. A pronounced middle phalange on the little finger, for example, might hint at a person's strong communication abilities. In contrast, a dominant base phalange on the thumb could suggest a person's willpower and determination.

The flexibility of fingers also holds significance. How a finger bends, especially if it can bend backward, can tell a lot about a person's adaptability and receptiveness to new experiences. Highly flexible fingers might be a sign of an individual who is open-minded and adaptable, whereas stiff fingers could point to someone more set in their ways.

The texture and consistency of the hand offer additional clues. The feel of the hand, be it soft, firm, dry, or moist, can provide insights into an individual's temperament. A soft hand might be indicative of a person who is emotionally attuned, while a firm hand could suggest someone more pragmatic.

Beyond the primary lines and individual symbols, the overall shape of the hand and fingers also plays a role in interpretations. A hand with a square palm and short fingers might belong to someone methodical and practical. In contrast, a hand with a long palm and elongated fingers could belong to someone more introspective.

For those keen on advancing their palmistry knowledge, several avenues can be explored.

We invite you to take up the trial to our Palm Reading Secrets Course, which you'll find links to at the front and back of this book.

Or Visit https://PalmReadingSecrets.com/bookbonus

Many workshops and courses are available, often led by experienced palmists. These sessions can provide both theoretical knowledge and practical hands-on experience.

The world of palmistry is rich in literature. Both classic texts and modern research can offer fresh perspectives and deeper understanding.

Seeking mentorship from seasoned palmists can be invaluable. They can provide personalized guidance, share their wealth of experience, and assist in navigating complex readings.

Regular practice is essential. Analyzing a variety of hands, understanding different patterns, and refining techniques can greatly enhance one's skills.

In essence, while the foundational principles of palmistry offer a robust starting point, the discipline is vast and layered. By exploring advanced techniques and committing to ongoing learning, one can unravel the deeper narratives etched in the lines and symbols of the hand, offering more profound and nuanced readings to those seeking insights.

Other Recommended Resources for Deepening Your Palmistry Knowledge

Palmistry is a captivating discipline that delves into the intricate patterns and symbols of the hand to reveal insights about an individual's life and destiny. For those passionate about deepening their understanding of this ancient art, there are numerous resources available. Here's a guide to some of the most recommended resources for expanding your palmistry knowledge.

Books are foundational resources for any subject, and palmistry is no exception, and of course we recommend Lions' Paws by Nellie Simmons Meier, if you can get your hands on a copy.

Online courses and workshops have become increasingly popular, offering interactive and flexible learning options. The International Institute of Hand Analysis, for instance, provides courses for all levels, from beginners to advanced practitioners. Platforms like Udemy and Coursera also host a variety of palmistry courses, often including video demonstrations and interactive exercises.

For those who prefer regular updates and discussions on the latest in palmistry, journals and magazines such as "The Journal of Palmistry" and "Hand Analysis Today" are invaluable. These publications feature articles, research findings, and interviews with leading experts in the field.

In today's digital age, there are also palmistry apps like "Palm Reading Insights" and "PalmistryHD" that offer quick and interactive hand analyses. While they can't replace in-depth study, they are useful tools for practice and quick references.

Mentorship is another avenue to consider. Learning under the guidance of an experienced palmist can provide personalized insights and feedback. This one-on-one interaction can be immensely beneficial in refining techniques and understanding nuances.

Study groups, either in-person or online, offer collaborative learning experiences. These groups provide a platform for discussions, sharing interpretations, and learning from diverse perspectives.

Conferences and retreats dedicated to palmistry offer immersive learning experiences. These events often feature workshops, lectures, and discussions led by renowned experts, providing attendees with a deeper understanding of specific topics and techniques.

Online forums and communities are also excellent resources. Websites like HandFacts and the Modern Hand Reading Forum host discussions, share experiences, and offer advice. Social media platforms, including Facebook and Reddit, have dedicated palmistry groups where enthusiasts from around the world connect and share their knowledge.

Understanding the history and cultural variations of palmistry can enrich one's practice. Exploring how palmistry has evolved over time and how different cultures interpret the hand can provide a broader perspective on this intricate art.

In essence, the world of palmistry is vast and layered, with a plethora of resources available for those eager to learn. Whether you're just starting out or looking to refine your skills, there's always something new to explore, understand, and incorporate into your practice. Embracing continuous learning and staying updated with the latest techniques and interpretations will ensure that your palmistry readings are insightful, accurate, and enlightening.

Building a Career in Palmistry

Palmistry, the time-honored art of interpreting the lines and formations of the hand, has fascinated humanity for centuries. Its enduring appeal lies in its ability to offer insights into an individual's character, potential, and life journey. For those drawn to this mystical discipline, pursuing a career in palmistry can be both personally fulfilling and professionally rewarding. Here's a detailed guide on how to navigate the path to becoming a successful palmist.

To begin with, a deep understanding of palmistry's foundational principles is paramount. This encompasses knowledge of the major and minor lines, the mounts, hand shapes, and the myriad of markings that can appear on the palm. While there's a wealth of information available, from ancient texts to modern manuals, it's vital to ensure that your foundational knowledge is sourced from reputable and authentic teachings.

Formal training in palmistry can provide a structured approach to learning. While many practitioners inherit the knowledge or learn through self-study, enrolling in a recognized course can offer a systematic curriculum and hands-on practice. Such courses often culminate in certification, which can lend credibility to your practice and inspire trust in potential clients.

However, theoretical knowledge alone isn't enough. Mastery in palmistry, like any other skill, is honed through consistent practice. Starting with readings for friends and family can provide a safe environment to apply your knowledge, receive feedback, and refine your technique. As you gain confidence, you can expand your readings to acquaintances and eventually, to the public.

As you conduct more sessions, it's beneficial to maintain a portfolio. With the permission of your clients, document your readings, especially those insights or predictions that manifest. This portfolio can serve as a testament to your expertise and can be instrumental in attracting new clients.

While many palmists begin their journey offering readings in informal settings, establishing a dedicated professional space can elevate your practice. This space, whether in your home or a rented premise, should exude calm and serenity, ensuring that your clients feel at ease during their sessions.

In our increasingly digital world, establishing an online presence can significantly boost your reach. A well-designed website, detailing your services, sharing testimonials, and offering a means of contact is essential. Additionally, leveraging social media platforms can help in building a community and attracting a wider audience. With the advent of technology, consider offering virtual readings, catering to clients globally.

The realm of palmistry is vast, and there's always more to learn. Stay abreast of the latest research, methodologies, and interpretations. Engaging with fellow palmists, attending workshops, and participating in conferences can further enhance your skills and understanding.

Ethics play a crucial role in palmistry. It's vital to approach each reading with honesty, compassion, and a genuine desire to assist. Avoid making predictions that could induce fear or make clients anxious. Emphasize the importance of free will and personal choices, ensuring clients understand that while the hand might offer insights, their decisions shape their destiny.

To further enrich your practice, consider learning related disciplines. Skills in tarot reading, astrology, or even numerology can complement your palmistry readings, offering clients a more holistic insight into their lives.

Pricing your services can be a delicate balance. Research what other palmists in your vicinity charge and set competitive rates. As your experience and clientele grow, you can reevaluate and adjust your pricing.

Lastly, networking can be invaluable. Connect with other professionals in the spiritual and metaphysical community.

Collaborations, referrals, and joint events can not only enhance your practice but also foster a sense of community.

Quickstart Guide to Start a Local Palm Reading Business

Embarking on the journey of starting a local palm reading business can be both an exciting and fulfilling venture. Palmistry, the ancient art of interpreting the lines on a person's palm to reveal their character and predict their future, has fascinated people for centuries. If you have a passion for palmistry and a desire to start your own business, this guide will walk you through the essential steps to establish a successful local palm reading business.

Step 1: Learn and Master Palm Reading

Before diving into the business aspect, it's crucial to have a solid understanding of palm reading. If you're not already an expert, consider taking courses, reading books, or finding a mentor in the field. Practice regularly and stay updated with the latest trends and techniques in palmistry.

Step 2: Define Your Business Model

Decide on the structure of your business. Will you operate from a physical location, offer readings at events, or provide services from your home? Consider starting small and scaling up as your client base grows. Also, think about the services you'll offer – will you provide only palm readings, or will you expand to other areas like tarot reading or astrology?

Consider approaching businesses in your town or city that sell books, crystals, clothing and alternative healing services, hair and nail salons, about offering your services as an added value to their customers either for a fee you pay them to have a table in their premises, promote special events with you, or a share of your earnings.

You may get a few establishments saying "no thanks" but you only need one to say yes to get you started.

Step 3: Legalize Your Business

Register your business according to your local laws. This may involve obtaining a business license, registering for taxes, and setting up a legal structure for your business (like an LLC). It's also wise to get liability insurance to protect your business.

Step 4: Set Up Your Workspace

If you're planning to read palms in a physical location, create a welcoming and comfortable space for your clients. The ambiance should be calming and professional. If you're working from home, ensure you have a quiet and private area for readings.

Step 5: Develop Your Brand

Create a strong brand identity. This includes choosing a business name, designing a logo, and establishing your brand's look and feel. Your brand should reflect the mystical and insightful nature of your services.

Step 6: Market Your Business

Utilize both online and offline marketing strategies to promote your palm reading business. Set up a professional website, engage on social media platforms, and consider local advertising in newspapers or local radio stations. Networking with other local businesses can also be beneficial.

Step 7: Set Your Pricing Structure

Research what other palmists in your area are charging and set competitive prices. You might start with lower prices to attract initial clients and increase your rates as you gain more experience and recognition.

Step 8: Offer Exceptional Customer Service

Word-of-mouth can be a powerful tool in this business. Provide exceptional service, and encourage satisfied clients to leave reviews or refer friends. Building a strong relationship with your clients can lead to repeat business and a loyal customer base.

Step 9: Expand Your Skills and Services

As your business grows, consider expanding your services. This could include offering classes on palmistry, selling related products, or expanding into other areas of fortune-telling or spiritual guidance.

Starting a local palm reading business requires a blend of skill in palmistry, business acumen, and a passion for helping others through spiritual guidance. With dedication, effective marketing, and exceptional customer service, your palm reading business can flourish, providing valuable insights to those seeking answers and guidance.

FAQs:

1. Do I need special certification to start a palm reading business?

- While certification is not legally required, having formal training or certification can enhance your credibility. Remember we've offered a free trial in our Palm Reading Secrets course to help build up your knowledge at https://PalmReadingSecrets.com/bookbonuses

2. How much can I expect to earn from a palm reading business?

- Earnings vary based on location, reputation, and the number of clients. It can range from a part-time income to a full-time salary.

3. Can I run a palm reading business online?

- Yes, many palmists offer readings via video calls, allowing them to reach a wider client base. We've provided some guidelines below for starting your business online.

4. What are the key challenges in starting a palm reading business?

- Challenges include building a client base, setting competitive prices, and distinguishing your services in a niche market.

Quickstart Guide to Starting a Palm Reading Business Online

Want to turn your palm reading skills into a successful online business? Follow this comprehensive guide and learn from the experiences of palmist entrepreneurs.

Embarking on the journey of starting an online palm reading business can be both exciting and rewarding. With the growing interest in mystical arts and personal well-being, the demand for palmistry services has seen a significant rise. This guide aims to navigate you through the process of transforming your palmistry skills into a thriving online venture.

Understanding the Industry

The palm reading industry, often intertwined with spiritual and self-help services, has found a robust market online. The digital platform offers a wider reach, allowing palmists to connect with clients globally. Understanding this market's dynamics is crucial for tailoring your services to meet the evolving needs of your audience.

Researching the Market and Competition

Begin by researching your market and understanding your competition. Identify your niche – are you focusing on career advice, love and relationships, or life path readings? Analyze what competitors offer and how you can differentiate your services. This step is vital in carving out your unique space in the palmistry market.

Establishing Your Brand and Unique Selling Proposition

Your brand is more than a logo; it's the experience and promise you offer your clients. Develop a unique selling proposition (USP) that sets you apart. Whether it's your reading style, specialized reports, or unique insights, your USP is what will attract clients to your service.

Building Your Online Presence

A professional website is your digital storefront. Ensure it's user-friendly, aesthetically pleasing, and SEO-optimized. Utilize social media platforms to market your services. Platforms like Instagram, Facebook, and TikTok can be powerful tools for showcasing your palmistry skills and connecting with potential clients.

Monetizing Your Palmistry Skills

There are various ways to monetize your palmistry skills online. You can offer personalized reading sessions, create and sell palmistry courses, or even sell related products like books or palm reading charts. Diversifying your income streams can help stabilize your business financially.

Legal and Administrative Considerations

It's essential to understand the legalities of running an online business. This includes registering your business, understanding tax obligations, and ensuring you comply with any online commerce regulations. Also, consider purchasing liability insurance to protect your business.

Pricing Your Services

Research standard rates in the industry but also consider your experience and the uniqueness of your services. Offering different pricing tiers can cater to a broader range of clients.

Marketing and Promotion

Effective marketing is key to attracting clients. Invest in digital marketing strategies like SEO, content marketing, and social media advertising. Collaborating with influencers or complementary businesses can also broaden your reach.

Providing Exceptional Customer Service

Exceptional customer service can set you apart in the online world. Be responsive, offer personalized experiences, and ensure your clients feel valued. Positive customer experiences often lead to referrals and repeat business.

Continuous Learning and Improvement

The world of palmistry is ever-evolving. Stay abreast of new trends, continuously hone your skills, and seek professional development opportunities. This not only enhances your service quality but also keeps you competitive.

Starting an online palm reading business offers a unique opportunity to turn your passion into a profitable venture. By understanding the market, establishing a strong brand, and effectively utilizing digital tools, you can build a successful online business. Remember, persistence, continuous learning, and adaptability are key to your success in the mystical world of palmistry.

FAQs:

1. Can I start an online palm reading business with no prior experience?

- Starting without experience is challenging but possible. Consider getting formal training or mentorship to build credibility.

2. How much can I earn from an online palm reading business?

- Earnings vary based on factors like reputation, pricing, and client base. Some successful online palmists earn a substantial income.

3. Are palm reading businesses legal?

- Yes, but ensure you comply with local business regulations and disclaimers about the entertainment nature of your services.

4. How can I attract clients to my online palm reading business?

- Utilize digital marketing, offer introductory rates, engage on social media, and gather positive reviews to attract clients.

In essence, a career in palmistry is a journey of continuous learning, practice, and connection. With dedication, empathy, and a genuine passion for the art, you can carve a niche for yourself in this ancient discipline, guiding countless individuals towards self-awareness and understanding.

CASE STUDY: MARY PICKFORD APRIL 11TH, 1933

America's Silent Film Icon

Born Gladys Louise Smith on April 8, 1892, in Toronto, Canada, Mary Pickford achieved legendary status as a silent film actress. Known as "America's Sweetheart," she captivated audiences with her expressive acting and endearing beauty.

Mary's career began in theater but quickly transitioned to film, where she became a sensation. She joined Biograph Company in 1910 and honed her craft under D.W. Griffith, becoming America's first movie star.

Famous for her roles in films like "The Poor Little Rich Girl" (1917), Mary connected with audiences on an emotional level. In 1919, she co-founded United Artists alongside her husband, Douglas Fairbanks, granting actors more creative control.

Mary Pickford and Douglas Fairbanks, both beloved stars, were known as Hollywood's "royal couple." Their legendary estate, Pickfair, became a symbol of Hollywood glamor and hosted countless luminaries of the era.

Mary was also a successful businesswoman, earning the title of the highest-paid actress of her time. Her talent earned her the first Academy Award for Best Actress in 1929 for "Coquette."

She seamlessly transitioned to sound films but retired in 1933, leaving behind a remarkable legacy. Mary Pickford remains an icon of Hollywood's early days, celebrated for her pioneering spirit, timeless charm, and her legendary partnership with Douglas Fairbanks at Pickfair.

Adapted from the character sketch from impressions of the hands of Mary Pickford on by Nellie Simmons Meier

Nellie Simmons Meier's journey to Hollywood in February 1933 marked her escape from the Midwestern blizzards to California's balmy climate and the opportunity to meet celebrated figures from various creative fields. At the top of her list of luminaries was Mary Pickford, affectionately known as "America's Sweetheart."

Arriving just a day before Mary Pickford's departure for Europe, Nellie's initial attempt at an interview was deferred. However, her hope was realized on April 11, 1933, when she secured an appointment with Mary Pickford at the famous Pickfair estate.

Pickfair had become a well-known symbol of Hollywood glamor, even for those who had not visited in person. Stepping inside, Nellie found the interior to be a perfect reflection of Mary Pickford's public image. The spacious rooms, interconnected by archways, led to the upper floor via an escalier d'honneur, where French elegance prevailed. Soft pearl gray velvet carpet adorned the floor, complemented by antique Oriental rugs. Paintings by French masters adorned paneled walls, and French furniture, covered in priceless tapestry, showcased an intimate knowledge of French architecture.

Nellie's journey continued as she descended into the music room, where glass doors opened to a breathtaking formal French garden. The garden featured various shades of pink, vibrant delphinium blues, purple, and lavender blooms, framed by mignonette and delicate Forget Me Not flowers. White lilies provided a stunning backdrop, with a fountain mirroring the surrounding beauty.

Invited into the library, Nellie marveled at the French book bindings on the crowded shelves. Intimate paintings adorned the walls, flanking a French marble fireplace. The desk's appointments featured tooled French leather, while an Aubusson rug graced the parquetry floor. French windows opened onto the veranda, enveloped by blooming rose bushes, honeysuckle, and wisteria, creating an unforgettable scene.

Nellie was then ushered into Mary Pickford's boudoir, which continued the harmonious and well-appointed theme of the lower floor. French windows led to typical balconies, offering views of the surrounding hillside. The boudoir, a spacious room with multiple windows, boasted the same carpet as downstairs and a welcoming wood-burning French fireplace. A beautiful painting of Mary Pickford's mother adorned the space, alongside framed photographs of her husband, Douglas Fairbanks, and close friends.

When Mary Pickford greeted Nellie with outstretched hands, the genuine warmth in her handshake and the sincerity in her demeanor instantly transported Nellie back to her early cinematic encounters with "America's Sweetheart." Although many are intrigued by the age of a famous personage, NSM thought this a minor detail compared to their achievements and the impressions they left behind.

While securing the impressions of Mary Pickford's hands, Nellie was struck by the satiny texture of her skin, the absence of typical signs of aging on the backs of her hands, and the firm, resilient feel of her palms—a reflection of both mental fortitude and an open, intelligent mind.

The graceful slope of her palms tapering to slender wrists revealed her inherent love for the finer, artistic aspects of life. The width beneath her fingers signaled a profound affinity for intellectual pursuits over physical exertion. Her thumbs, while unusually long, displayed a measured flexibility. She could maintain an amiable and poised demeanor in public, yet those who aimed to venture deeper into her heart found that congeniality, shared outlooks on life, and aligned ideals were prerequisites.

The elongated first or nail phalange, representing willpower, spoke volumes about her relentless dedication to her objectives. Obstacles failed to daunt her, and opposition merely fortified her resolve. She epitomized the adage that "an ounce of opposition is worth a whole pound of incentive." The inward curve of the second phalange of logic or reason hinted at a brilliant intellect. Although she couldn't always suppress her desires and sympathies, as evident in the mount at the base of her thumb, she had the capacity to let cold reason steer her course. The length of her fingers indicated meticulous attention to detail, softened by a smoothness that showcased her inspirational nature, sparing her from fussiness or excessive concern over domestic minutiae.

The first or nail phalange on all her fingers reflected a conscientious respect for the rights of others and a dedicated commitment to her undertakings. Her first finger, Jupiter, denoted executive acumen and ambition, while its tip hinted at rapid perception. The relative length of the first and second phalange indicated a harmonious balance between mercy and justice. She wasn't given to emotional generosity, but her acts of benevolence were guided by a deep understanding of others' needs and a commitment to address the root causes of their circumstances.

In her second finger, Saturn, the shape and tip of the nail phalange hinted at an innate optimism and a hopeful outlook on life that enabled her to emerge from profound grief, disappointments, and bitter disillusionment with a clear mental perspective and a keen appreciation of life's rewards. Within the third finger, Apollo, the nail phalange's shape revealed her recognition of the necessity of technique in realizing her artistic visions. The length of the first phalange, in comparison to the second, underscored her quick recognition of the technical foundation, prioritizing it over emotional or colorful expression in the realm of creative art.

In her fourth finger, Mercury, the outward flare from the hand showcased her independence of thought and action, a trait that contributed significantly to her remarkable persona. The pointed tip indicated her gift for effective expression, while the finger's length spoke to her diplomatic finesse, which not only helped her navigate trying circumstances but also allowed her to maintain her composure and conquer unjust criticism.

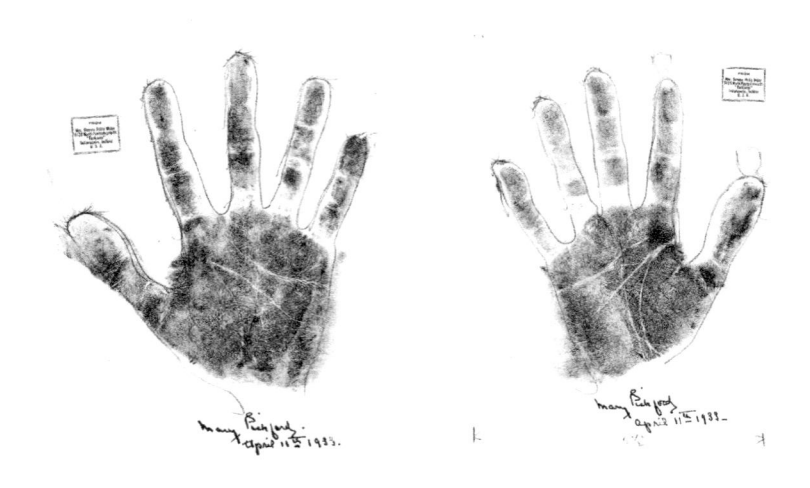

CHAPTER 13

Beyond Palm Reading: Integrating Numerology and Astrology

Palmistry, with its deep roots in ancient wisdom, offers profound insights into an individual's personality, life path, and potential. However, the world of divination is vast and interconnected, and exploring additional tools such as numerology and astrology can enrich our understanding of the human psyche. In this chapter, we will delve into the intriguing realm of numerology and astrology, and explore how they complement and enhance the practice of palmistry.

Finding Connections Between Hand Shapes and Numerology

Numerology, the study of numbers and their spiritual significance, has long been revered as a powerful tool for self-discovery and understanding. By examining the numeric vibrations present in an individual's birth date, we can gain deeper insights into their personality traits, strengths, and challenges.

Incorporating numerology into palmistry creates a symbiotic relationship between the two divinatory arts. The unique hand shape and its elemental composition, as revealed in palmistry, often align with specific numerological vibrations. For instance, individuals with an earthy hand shape may resonate strongly with the number 4, representing stability and practicality, while those with an air hand shape may align with the number 7, symbolizing intellect and introspection.

Combining hand shape analysis with numerology enables us to paint a more comprehensive picture of the individual's inherent qualities and tendencies. It empowers seekers with greater self-awareness and provides them with valuable tools to navigate life's challenges and opportunities.

By intertwining the wisdom of palmistry and numerology, we unlock a deeper understanding of the seeker's destiny and life path, allowing for a holistic approach to self-discovery and personal growth.

The Influence of Astrology in Palmistry

Zodiac Signs and Their Impact on Palm Lines and Characteristics

Astrology, the study of celestial bodies and their influence on human lives, provides profound insights into an individual's inherent traits, behavioral patterns, and destiny. Each zodiac sign carries unique qualities and characteristics, which manifest in an individual's personality and life experiences.

Illustrations: Illuminating Palmistry Concepts

Illustrations serve as invaluable visual aids that clarify complex palmistry concepts and help readers grasp the intricacies of hand analysis. From the arrangement of the lines to the positioning of the mounts, illustrations provide clarity and visual coherence.

In palmistry books and resources, illustrations showcase various hand shapes, line patterns, and mount positions, guiding readers through the process of hand analysis step by step. These illustrations often feature different hand types and examples of specific line configurations, offering readers a range of real-life scenarios for better comprehension.

Illustrations also highlight the diverse interpretations of various palmistry features. For instance, a broken head line may indicate a shift in career focus for one individual, while for another, it may symbolize periods of mental restlessness. By presenting these diverse scenarios, illustrations empower readers to develop their interpretive skills and expand their understanding of the multifaceted nature of palmistry.

The Role of Visual Learning in Palmistry Education

Visual learning plays a fundamental role in palmistry education, as it allows individuals to grasp complex concepts more effectively and retain information with greater ease. Palmistry, being a discipline that requires attention to minute details and subtle variations, benefits greatly from visual aids that highlight these nuances.

Through a combination of written explanations and visual representations, individuals can engage both their analytical and creative faculties, enhancing their overall learning experience. Visual learning also fosters a deeper connection with the subject matter, making it more relatable and memorable.

Virtual Learning Platforms and Interactive Tools

In the digital age, virtual learning platforms and interactive tools have revolutionized palmistry education. Online courses, video tutorials, and interactive hand analysis software offer immersive learning experiences that cater to diverse learning styles.

Virtual learning platforms allow learners to access a vast repository of palmistry resources, including handprints from individuals of different age groups, backgrounds, and cultural origins. These digital resources provide students with a broader perspective and exposure to a wide range of hand features, enhancing their ability to interpret various hand types and patterns.

Interactive hand analysis software offers a unique hands-on approach to palmistry education. Learners can virtually mark the lines, mounts, and features on a digital handprint, guided by real-time feedback and interpretations. This interactive experience empowers learners to refine their analysis skills and build confidence in their readings.

Embracing the Visual Dimension of Palmistry

As we explore the world of palmistry, handprints and illustrations serve as indispensable tools that enrich our understanding and appreciation of the art and science of reading palms. These visual aids provide valuable insights into an individual's unique characteristics, traits, and life experiences, guiding us on a journey of self-discovery and personal growth.

In combination with textual descriptions, handprints offer a tangible connection to each person's life story, and illustrations shed light on the diverse interpretations of palmistry features. With the aid of virtual learning platforms and interactive tools, palmistry education becomes more accessible and engaging, allowing learners to delve deeper into the intricate world of hand analysis.

As we embrace the visual dimension of palmistry, let us remember that each handprint is a testament to the vastness of human diversity and the richness of individual journeys. Whether we are professional palmists or individuals seeking self-understanding, handprints and illustrations serve as portals to the soul, unveiling the tapestry of life etched into the palms of our hands. Through the visual language of palmistry, we embark on a profound quest for knowledge, wisdom, and connection with ourselves and the world around us.

The Future of Palmistry

Innovations in Palmistry And Technological advancements in hand analysis

As we venture into the future, the art and science of palmistry continue to evolve and adapt, embracing technological advancements that enhance the practice of hand analysis. From cutting-edge imaging techniques to sophisticated artificial intelligence, the future of palmistry holds exciting possibilities that will revolutionize the way we understand and interpret the intricate lines and features of the human hand.

High-Resolution Imaging: The Power of Precision

Advancements in imaging technology have already made a significant impact on various fields of science and medicine, and palmistry is no exception. High-resolution imaging techniques, such as 3D scanning and infrared imaging, offer unparalleled precision in capturing the minute details of an individual's hand.

These advanced imaging technologies enable palmists to analyze the handprint with unprecedented accuracy, enhancing the detection and interpretation of subtle line variations, patterns, and shapes. The depth and clarity of 3D hand models provide a deeper insight into the hand's contours and surface texture, leading to more comprehensive and detailed readings.

Virtual Reality (VR) Hand Analysis: An Immersive Experience

Virtual reality (VR) technology is poised to revolutionize palmistry education and practice by offering an immersive experience for both palmists and clients. Through VR hand analysis, learners can interact with virtual handprints, mark lines and mounts, and receive real-time feedback on their interpretations.

For clients, VR hand analysis provides an engaging and interactive experience as they explore the unique characteristics of their hands in a virtual environment. The ability to manipulate and rotate the virtual handprint offers a dynamic and personalized encounter with the art of palmistry.

Artificial Intelligence (AI) and Machine Learning: Expanding Interpretations

The integration of artificial intelligence (AI) and machine learning in palmistry holds immense potential to augment the accuracy and scope of hand analysis. AI algorithms can analyze vast databases of handprints, identifying patterns and correlations that may not be apparent to the human eye.

By learning from millions of handprints and their corresponding life experiences, AI-driven palmistry tools can provide more nuanced interpretations and personalized insights. These tools have the potential to identify trends and associations between certain hand features and specific personality traits or life events, enriching the depth and breadth of palmistry readings.

Biometric Palm Analysis: Identity Verification and Beyond

Biometric palm analysis is an emerging area of research that explores the use of hand features for identity verification and authentication. In addition to traditional biometric methods such as fingerprint and facial recognition, palm biometrics offer a unique and promising approach to identity verification.

The patterns of lines and features on an individual's palm are highly distinctive and remain relatively stable throughout life. As a result, palm biometrics can serve as a reliable and secure method of identity verification, potentially finding applications in various industries, including finance, healthcare, and security.

Global Collaboration and Digital Platforms

In the digital age, palmistry enthusiasts and professionals from around the world are coming together on digital platforms to exchange knowledge, share handprints, and collaborate on research projects. Online communities and forums allow palmists to connect with peers, discuss findings, and seek mentorship, fostering a global network of palmistry practitioners.

Digital platforms also facilitate the sharing of handprints and case studies, contributing to a growing database of palmistry resources. This global collaboration not only enriches the collective understanding of hand analysis but also promotes a sense of unity and camaraderie among palmistry enthusiasts.

Ethical Considerations in Technological Advancements

As palmistry embraces technological innovations, it is essential to navigate ethical considerations and maintain a responsible approach to hand analysis. Client consent, privacy, and data security must be prioritized when utilizing advanced imaging and AI-driven tools.

Additionally, palmists must be vigilant in avoiding over-reliance on technology at the expense of their own intuitive insights and expertise. Technology should complement the artistry of palmistry, not replace it. Striking a balance between human intuition and technological precision is crucial for maintaining the authenticity and integrity of the palmistry practice.

Embracing the Future: Empowering Palmistry

The future of palmistry is one of limitless possibilities, fueled by advancements in technology and a growing interest in self-discovery and personal growth. As hand analysis continues to evolve, it remains rooted in its timeless essence as a profound tool for understanding the individuality and complexity of human beings.

In embracing the future of palmistry, we open ourselves to a world of exploration and discovery. High-resolution imaging, virtual reality experiences, AI-driven interpretations, biometric applications, and global collaboration hold the promise of expanding the horizons of hand analysis, empowering both palmists and clients on their respective journeys of self-discovery.

As we look forward to the unfolding future of palmistry, let us cherish the ancient wisdom that the human hand holds and the boundless potential for growth and transformation it represents. The convergence of art, science, and technology offers a bright horizon for palmistry, ensuring that this timeless practice continues to inspire and guide generations to come.

Palmistry as a Journey of Self-Discovery

Embracing Self-Exploration

Recognize the transformative potential of palmistry as a tool for self-awareness and personal growth. Understand that the knowledge gained from reading one's own hand can be empowering and enlightening.

Integrating Palmistry into Daily Life

Discover how to integrate palmistry insights into your daily routine, making use of the newfound knowledge to navigate life's challenges, improve relationships, and make informed decisions.

As you delve into the world of palmistry in this chapter, remember that it is a journey of continuous learning and exploration. Each hand is a unique reflection of its owner's experiences and personality. With an open heart and a curious mind, you will unlock the secrets held within the lines of the human hand and uncover the profound wisdom that awaits you.

CASE STUDY: WALTER HUSTON

Walter Huston (1884-1950) was a Canadian-born American actor renowned for his versatility in theater and film, spanning musical comedy to high drama. Initially an engineer, Huston debuted on the Toronto stage in 1902 and in New York in 1905. He returned to acting in 1909, performing with his second wife, Bayonne Whipple, as a song-and-dance team until 1924.

Huston's notable Broadway roles included Marshall Pitt in "Mr. Pitt" (1924) and Ephraim Cabot in "Desire Under the Elms" (1924). He married actress Nan Sunderland the same year. His performance in "Dodsworth" (1934) earned him critical acclaim and an Academy Award nomination for the film adaptation (1936).

With the advent of sound films, Huston primarily focused on cinema but continued stage work. He appeared in over 50 films, including notable roles in "Abraham Lincoln" (1930), "Law and Order" (1932), and "All That Money Can Buy" (1941). His performance in "The Treasure of the Sierra Madre" (1948), directed by his son John Huston, won him an Academy Award for Best Supporting Actor.

Adapted from the character sketch from impressions of the hands of Walter Huston by Nellie Simmons Meier

In Hollywood, NSM was invited to read Huston's hands, revealing traits through observation during a car ride. His square, firm palm indicated a positive nature and careful deliberation in decision-making. His smooth fingers to the second joint showed restrained inspirational qualities, balanced by a desire for material law and order. His conservative expression of opinions and tenacity in viewpoints were evident in the small flares of his thumb and fingers.

Huston's wide space between his life and headline showed initiative and independence, tempered by experience. His rounded mount of Venus reflected vitality, endurance, and a deep, tender loyalty to loved ones and friends. His double-jointed thumbs, combined with his vitality and careful decision-making, contributed to his success in his profession.

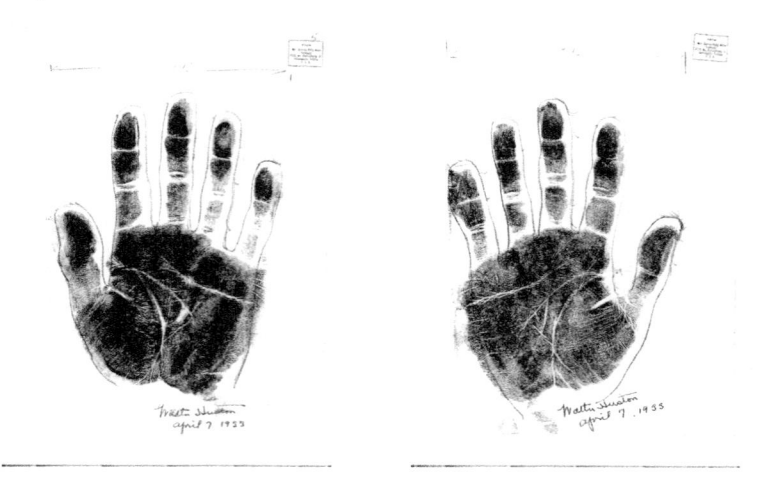

CHAPTER 14

Preserving the Art of Palmistry.

Encouraging the Practice for Future Generations

As the world progresses with rapid technological advancements and scientific discoveries, ancient arts like palmistry risk being overshadowed and forgotten. However, preserving the art of palmistry is crucial, as it represents a valuable and time-honored tradition of self-discovery and personal insight. Encouraging the practice of palmistry for future generations ensures that this profound and transformative art continues to thrive and inspire seekers of knowledge and wisdom.

Embracing Cultural Heritage and Tradition

Preserving the art of palmistry begins with recognizing its significance as a part of our cultural heritage and tradition. Across various civilizations and cultures, palmistry has played a pivotal role in understanding human nature and unlocking the mysteries of the soul. Embracing this rich history allows us to appreciate the deep wisdom and universal truths embedded in the lines and features of the human hand.

By sharing stories and experiences of palmistry from different cultural perspectives, we foster a sense of cultural appreciation and diversity. This helps in keeping the practice relevant and meaningful, ensuring that future generations recognize its value as a treasure trove of ancient knowledge and insights.

Promoting Palmistry Education

Education is the cornerstone of preserving any art or tradition. Encouraging palmistry education at schools, workshops, and online platforms provides opportunities for aspiring palmists to delve into this ancient practice and refine their skills. Palmistry courses can be designed to cater to learners of all ages and backgrounds, allowing them to explore the intricacies of hand analysis and develop a profound connection with the art.

Palmistry educators and mentors play a vital role in passing on their expertise to the next generation of palmists. By sharing their knowledge, experiences, and techniques, they empower young learners to embrace the artistry and science of palmistry with confidence and dedication.

Promoting Ethical and Responsible Practice

Preserving the art of palmistry also necessitates promoting ethical and responsible practice. Palmistry practitioners should adhere to a code of ethics that emphasizes respect for client privacy, informed consent, and confidentiality. Ethical guidelines ensure that the art of palmistry is practiced with integrity and empathy, fostering trust and credibility in the field.

By upholding these ethical principles, palmists set an example for future generations, emphasizing the importance of compassion, empathy, and professionalism in their practice. This not only preserves the art's reputation but also cultivates a nurturing and supportive environment for seekers of palmistry guidance.

Advocating for Recognition and Validation

Palmistry has often faced skepticism and skepticism from skeptics and critics who dismiss it as pseudoscience or superstition. Advocating for recognition and validation of palmistry as a valuable tool for self-discovery and personal growth is essential to preserving its integrity and relevance.

Through research, publications, and collaborations with scientific communities, palmists can present empirical evidence and case studies that demonstrate the efficacy and accuracy of hand analysis. By engaging in respectful dialogues with skeptics and open-minded individuals, palmists can bridge the gap between science and spirituality, fostering a greater appreciation for the art's wisdom and insights.

Nurturing a Sense of Wonder and Curiosity

Preserving the art of palmistry involves nurturing a sense of wonder and curiosity about the human hand's complexity and the stories it holds. Encouraging individuals to explore their own hands and reflect on the lines and features fosters a sense of self-awareness and introspection. This process kindles a deeper connection with the art and reinforces its significance in understanding oneself and others.

Educational resources, such as books, articles, and documentaries, can play a crucial role in inspiring curiosity and fascination with palmistry. These resources celebrate the art's beauty and intricacy, appealing to both novices and seasoned enthusiasts, and cultivating a passion for the art that transcends generations.

CASE STUDY: PU LUN PRINCE OF CHINA

Royal Prince Pu Lun, Future Emperor of China, Guest of Indianapolis, Ind. Week of May 17th, 1904.

Pu Lun Prince of China

Pu Lun (also known as Prince Pu Lun), born in 1880, was a notable figure in late Qing Dynasty China. He was a member of the Aisin Gioro clan, the imperial family of the Qing Dynasty, and a distant cousin of the last Emperor, Puyi. His full title was Prince of the First Rank Pu Lun, reflecting his high status within the imperial hierarchy.

Pu Lun's life intersected with a period of significant turmoil and change in China. The Qing Dynasty, which had ruled for over two centuries, was in decline during his lifetime, facing both internal rebellions and external pressures from foreign powers. Pu Lun, however, was known more for his cultural and diplomatic activities than for direct involvement in the political struggles of the time.

One of the most notable episodes in Pu Lun's life was his visit to the United States in 1904. He was officially invited to attend the Louisiana Purchase Exposition, also known as the St. Louis World's Fair. His visit was part of a broader effort by the Qing government to strengthen diplomatic ties and modernize the country through exposure to Western advancements. During his visit, Pu Lun was received by President Theodore Roosevelt, an event that symbolized the growing interaction between China and the United States.

Pu Lun was known for his interest in Western culture and technology, which was relatively unusual for Chinese princes of his time. He was seen as a symbol of a new, more open China, and his visit to the United States was widely covered in the American press. He was noted for his good command of English, his elegant manners, and his interest in various aspects of American life, from technology to sports.

After the fall of the Qing Dynasty in 1911 and the establishment of the Republic of China, many members of the imperial family faced uncertain futures. However, Pu Lun managed to navigate these changes, though details about his later life are less well-documented. He passed away in 1924, leaving behind a legacy as one of the more outward-looking and internationally engaged members of the Qing imperial family.

Pu Lun's life and activities, particularly his visit to the United States, provide a fascinating glimpse into the interactions between China and the West during a pivotal period in Chinese history. His story reflects the complexities and contradictions of a time when China was grappling with tradition and modernity, and with its place in a rapidly changing world.

Adapted from the character sketch from impressions of the hands of Pu Lun, Prince of China, by Nellie Simmons Meier

Prince Pu-Lun's hands reflected a personality that appreciated comfort, luxury, and the arts while also valuing practicality. His fingers' length suggested attention to detail, with a knack for understanding things deeply. However, the developed second joint indicated a tendency to delve beneath the surface before accepting things at face value. Interestingly, this revealed a need for others to maintain order around him rather than his personal orderliness.

The length of his first finger indicated a desire for power and leadership, combined with a sense of justice and mercy rarely seen in an Oriental leader. His fourth finger hinted at diplomatic prowess, and the flexibility of his thumbs showcased a unique ability to govern with grace and adaptability. Those under his rule benefited from his intuitive understanding of their abilities and limitations, as seen in the mound opposite his thumb.

His slightly curved fingers and thumbs indicated curiosity in all aspects of life, from the manufacturing of ice cream and beer to cultural, artistic, and mechanical pursuits. However, his left thumb's flexibility and pointed tip suggested a restless, impatient nature in his youth, while the stiffness of his right thumb revealed his disciplined efforts to maintain a calm and dignified exterior.

The lengths of the thumb's phalanges indicated a balanced will and a willingness to engage in logical arguments, showing a broad mentality open to reason. His lifeline suggested robust health and vitality. Tragically, Prince Pu-Lun was decapitated in July 1912 during the Manchu warlords' brief victory, before they were ousted and the Chinese Republic established.

Indeed, his hands provide a glimpse into the complexities of his life, including its tragic end, inviting further exploration by students to find it in his palms.

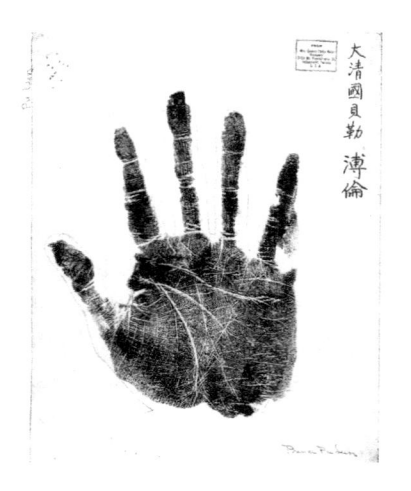

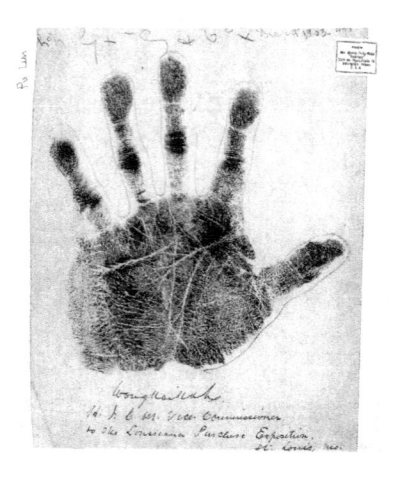

CHAPTER 15

Acknowledging the Legacy of Nellie Simmons Meier

In the realm of palmistry, one name that stands out with utmost reverence and respect is Nellie Simmons Meier (1886-1971). Acknowledging her legacy is essential as she played a pivotal role in elevating palmistry as a respected field of study and practice.

A Trailblazer in Palmistry

Nellie Simmons Meier was a remarkable figure in the world of palmistry, and her contributions have left an indelible mark on the field. Born in Brooklyn, New York, she exhibited an early fascination with the art of palmistry and embarked on a journey of deep exploration.

She dedicated her life to studying and refining her palmistry techniques, continuously seeking to understand the profound intricacies of hand analysis. Through her dedication and hard work, she became a pioneering figure in the field, recognized for her accuracy and insight.

The Wisdom of the "Message of the Hands"

Nellie Simmons Meier's magnum opus, "Lions' Paws," stands as a testament to her knowledge and expertise. Published in 1937, this seminal work provided a comprehensive and insightful guide to the practice of palmistry.

In "Lions' Paws," Meier not only delved into the art's scientific aspects but also emphasized the importance of intuition and the development of a personal connection with the hands being read. Her teachings highlighted the need for palmists to approach their craft with empathy, understanding, and humility.

Nurturing the Practice of Palmistry

Throughout her life, Nellie Simmons Meier shared her wisdom and insights with aspiring palmists, nurturing the practice of palmistry for generations to come. Her dedication to mentoring and teaching others underscores her commitment to preserving the art and passing on her expertise.

Her influence continues to inspire modern palmists, encouraging them to approach palmistry as a transformative and enriching practice. By acknowledging Meier's legacy, we honor the profound contributions she made to the field of palmistry.

An Enduring Legacy

Nellie Simmons Meier's work remains relevant and influential in contemporary palmistry. Her emphasis on combining science and intuition, along with her appreciation for the uniqueness of each individual, continues to shape the way palmists approach their readings.

Her legacy serves as a reminder of the artistry and sensitivity involved in palmistry. As aspiring palmists embark on their own journeys of self-discovery and exploration, they draw inspiration from Meier's commitment to ethical and compassionate practice.

Embracing palmistry as a life-enriching tool empowers individuals to embark on a journey of self-discovery, personal growth, and empowerment. By exploring the messages conveyed by our hands, we gain insights into our personalities, strengths, and potential paths in life.

Moreover, acknowledging the legacy of pioneers like Nellie Simmons Meier highlights the significance of preserving the art of palmistry for future generations. Her dedication to the practice and her contributions to the field continue to inspire and guide modern palmists, ensuring that this ancient art thrives as a timeless source of wisdom and understanding. By embracing palmistry's transformative potential and honoring its heritage, we nurture a practice that continues to enrich the lives of seekers of knowledge and self-awareness.

As we delve into the depths of palmistry, we encounter a wealth of knowledge and insights that transcend time and cultural boundaries. The fusion of palmistry with other disciplines, such as numerology and astrology, opens new vistas of understanding and adds layers of richness to the exploration of self.

In the following chapters, we will explore how palmistry intertwines with numerology and astrology, creating a comprehensive system of self-discovery. By integrating these disciplines, we gain a holistic understanding of the self, the connections between our past, present, and future, and the interplay between our inherent traits and the cosmic energies that shape our journey.

The synthesis of palmistry, numerology, and astrology offers a profound tapestry of knowledge, unveiling the intricacies of our existence and our unique place in the universe. As we embark on this exciting journey of exploration, we will discover how these disciplines converge to unlock the secrets hidden within our hands and the celestial dance that influences our lives. Through this integrated approach, we embrace the multidimensionality of our being and embrace the vastness of the human experience.

As we delve into the mysteries of palmistry, numerology, and astrology, we encourage you to approach this exploration with an open mind and a curious heart. The journey of self-discovery is one of constant growth and revelation, and each step brings us closer to the essence of our true selves.

Let us continue on this path of enlightenment, guided by the wisdom of the ancient sages and the visionaries who have illuminated the way before us. Through the merging of palmistry, numerology, and astrology, we embrace the beauty of interconnectedness and unveil the infinite possibilities that lie within the palm of our hands and the vast expanse of the cosmos.

So, dear seeker of knowledge, let us embark on this transformative quest together, as we unravel the enigmatic language of the palms, decipher the sacred numbers, and interpret the cosmic influences that shape our lives. The journey of self-discovery awaits, and the keys to unlock the door to inner wisdom and self-awareness are within reach.

May this journey bring you profound insights, empowerment, and a deep connection with the intricate symphony of life's cosmic dance. As we navigate the realms of palmistry, numerology, and astrology, we are reminded of the profound words of the poet Rumi: "You are not a drop in the ocean. You are the entire ocean in a drop."

Let us embrace the infinite wisdom and boundless potential that reside within each of us, for it is through this exploration that we truly discover the vastness of our being and the magnitude of our human experience. Welcome to the wondrous world of palmistry, numerology, and astrology—a journey of self-discovery that knows no bounds.

EXCLUSIVE BONUS OFFER FOR READERS

Unlock the Mysteries of Palmistry with Our Special Offer!

Dear Reader of **Palm Reading Secrets**,

You've embarked on an exciting journey into the world of palmistry with our book. Are you ready to dive even deeper? We have an exclusive invitation just for you!

Introducing the "Palm Reading Secrets Course" – Your Gateway to Mastering Palmistry

Experience Palmistry Like Never Before

Join our comprehensive online course designed to take your palm reading skills to the next level. Whether you're a curious beginner or an aspiring palmist, this course is the perfect next step in your journey.

Why Join the Palm Reading Secrets Course?

1. **In-Depth Training**: Delve into advanced techniques and interpretations that go beyond the book. Learn to read palms with greater accuracy and insight.

2. **Expert Guidance:** Be guided by seasoned palmists. Our instructors bring years of experience and will share their secret tips and tricks with you.

3. **More Insights from Celebrity Palm Reader Nellie Simmons Meier:** Access hundreds of palm reading sessions meticulously detailed by Mrs Meier to practice and perfect your skills.

4. **Exclusive Community Access:** Connect with fellow palmistry enthusiasts. Share readings, gain feedback, and grow together in a supportive environment.

Special Bonus Offer – Free Trial Access!

As a valued reader of "Palm Reading Secrets," we're thrilled to offer you a FREE trial to access the **Palm Reading Secrets** Course.

Your Free Trial Includes:

- Full access to the first module of the course.
- Early bird discounts on the full course upon completion of your trial.

Embrace Your Palmistry Passion

This is your chance to enhance your understanding and skills in palmistry. With our course, you'll gain the confidence to read palms like a pro and uncover the secrets hidden in the lines of the hand.

Don't Miss This Opportunity!

Claim your free trial now and continue your journey into the fascinating world of palmistry.

Your path to palmistry mastery awaits. Join the Palm Reading Secrets Course today and unlock the full potential of your palm reading abilities!

From Curiosity to Mastery to Earning!

Whether you're a beginner or someone with a budding interest in palmistry, this course is your comprehensive mentoring program. It takes you from the basics of understanding palm reading lines to mastering the art of interpretation. Imagine the possibility of turning this newfound skill into a thriving business, offering insights and guidance to others.

LEARN PALM READING SECRETS
A Beginner's Guide to Palmistry
ROZ LOCKE, Ph.D.

BONUS FREE TRIAL MEMBERSHIP

Discover the Secrets Revealed by Roz Locke, Ph.D., in her Exploration of Celebrity Palmist Nellie Simmons Meier's Work.

Here's how to get access:
https://PalmReadingSecrets.com/ReaderBonuses

Printed in Great Britain
by Amazon